Arthur Woorster

Random Rhymes

Arthur Woorster

Random Rhymes

ISBN/EAN: 9783337427931

Printed in Europe, USA, Canada, Australia, Japan

Cover: Foto ©Thomas Meinert / pixelio.de

More available books at **www.hansebooks.com**

RANDOM RHYMES

BY THE

"Pet Lariat"

WASHINGTON, D. C.
1882.

To the two horsemen who bestowed upon me the euphonious soubriquet that embellishes the memorable "Horse-meat Expedition," these verses are (without permission) dedicated by the Poet Lariat.

to the other survivors of

PREFACE.

Should you ask me why I've written lines like these,
  bereft of beauty;—
Utterly devoid of wisdom, and of cleverness and
  genius;
Naught herein to interest you, to amuse or entertain
  you—
I should answer, I should tell you: Just because it
  pleased my fancy!
Just because "I had a mind to!"
Should you then wax warm and "huffy" at the curt-
  ness of my answer,
At my reply, curt and churlish; and should ask in
  accents frigid,
In a vein denoting satire:—Do you deem such
  doggerel *poetry?*
I should calmly make rejoinder:—Was your grand-
  mamma a monkey?
Or *votre père* a Gila-monster, that you thus parade
  unaided such a doleful lack of *sabe?*

Having courteously responded—to your possible
  inquiries—
I— most humbly and sincerely, write the name
  bequeathed unto me.
  "Poet Lariat."

CONTENTS.

	PAGE
TO THE WILD WEST	1
CLEOPATRA'S PROTEST	7
A PROPHECY	12
AN EPISODE	20
IN MEMORIAM	24
CUSTER'S FUNERAL	26
A VICTIM OF FATE	28
'TWAS AU REVOIR	36
JEANETTE'S ANSWER	38
ALONE AT THE SPRINGS	40
JIM LEE	43
CHARITY	53
AT THE GRAVE OF C. W. D.	55
MEMORIAL VERSES	57
TO M. D. G.	59
RETRIBUTION	61
INTROSPECTION	67
TO N. D.	69
R. M.	72
W. H. B.	73
DISSOLUTION	74

CONTENTS.

	PAGE
The Doomed Stag	76
A Blossom	81
A Scene in a Cemetery	84
Retrospection	87
To B. B.	89
Jimjam Ike on Reformation	91
To B.	97
Poverty	101
The Debutante	103
To M. C. F.	106
A Quandary	109
A Life drama	111
"Come In;" or the Six Seasons	113
The Meadow-Lark	115

PARODIES.

Preface	121
Prologue to Slim Buttes	123
Slim Buttes	133
Antony	135
Car-ma-nee	141
To M. C. W.	145
The Iron-Bound Bucker	147
An Idle	150
"It was the Cat"	151
Peace Policy	153

RANDOM RHYMES.

TO THE WILD WEST.

Take me back to my love, to my glorious West!
   Where the sun sinks down in its flame-lit skies;
   Where he bids good night to the toil and sighs
Of the laboring world, and sinks to rest
In his cradle of gold he loves the best,
   Beyond the scope of the East's cold eyes.

Take me back to my West! to my early love,
   With her reaching plains and mountains of gold,
   That guard her borders like sentinels bold;
That loom in their grandeur beyond, above
The clouds that flit like a snow-white dove,
   And wrap their heights in their vapory fold.

Take me back again to her reaching plains,
   Whose limits are lost in the sky's fond kiss,
   As it stoops with blushes to drink the bliss
That flows with a flood through her wild warm veins,
Which are free from the fulsome taints and stains
   That are born in the blood of a clime like this!

Take me back to her plains where the cactus flowers
   In colors which none save God can paint—
   With blossoms so perfect and never a taint!
To her sable hills where the pine-tree towers,
To her Rosebud Vale and her wild-formed bowers,
   To that Eden where never was heard complaint!

Take me back again to her cañons, so deep
   You wonder if even your God can tell
   If they reach to Heaven or sink to Hell,
As silent they lie in their endless sleep!
While in rapture and terror you bend and weep,
   And hide your thought in its innermost cell.

Take me back to the life that beats in the breast
   Of her rivers that flow o'er their beds of gold!
   To their babble and laughter, as on they roll
To the great calm sea that fringes the West—
From its Southern edge to its Northern crest,
   Where their secrets are hid 'neath its bosom's fold.

Take me back to the rest, to those kingly dreams
   That lived in my sleep when my head was laid
   On my saddle seat, 'neath the spreading shade
Of the cottonwood boughs that arch her streams,
While the moon through her lattice of stars shed beams
   That lent to my vision her mystic aid!

Take me back again to my playmates wild!
   To the tender fawn and the graceful doe—
   To the lordling elk, and the buffalo,
That fed from my hand like a trustful child,
And seemed to speak with their eyes so mild
   They would soften the heart of a savage foe!

TO THE WILD WEST.

To the turkey-wild, and the plumèd quail,
    To the plover, and pheasant and burnished dove,
    That whistled and called and cooed their love,
When the day would dawn, or the night would pale ;
To the lark, whose carol would never fail
    To tell me the sun in the East did move !

Take me back to her monarchs, her mighty men,
    Her moulds of the noblest work of God,
    Who pressed the turf of her virgin sod
When she was unborn to the East, and when
Her wonders and riches were hid from its ken,
    And barred from its sight by a dazzling rod !

Her rugged frontiersmen with hearts as great
    As that which throbbed in the land they sought ;
    Those heroes who struggled and battled and fought
Their path to her heart, undeterred by the fate
That frowned on their daring and bade them wait ;
    But onward they pressed for the West, or naught !

Take me back to the comrades and scouts I knew
    In her dear old land in the cycles dead,
    When into the depths of her soul we led,
And journeyed together her full length through—
Nor grief, nor sorrow, nor trouble knew,
    Save the rightful shot of the foeman red !

I know you are crude, but I love you West
    In your own wild way as I saw you first,
    When my youthful heart was for love athirst !
And then God made you, and who knows best ?
What mortal dare say which is best or worst,
    The man-made East, or the God-made West ?

But my love, my love! I fear you will wed
   With the cold, proud East who is wrinkled and old;
   You will give him your freshness and beauty and gold,
And get but his science and art instead;
And your velvety breast where I've pillowed my head,
   Will be torn by the ploughshare, and staked and sold!

Your mountains and hills shall be tunneled through,
   So the smoking horse that is fed by steam
   Can dash through their centre with frightful scream,
And fill them with terror—so strange and new;
And shafts shall be sunk in their sides, and you
   Will awake too late from your fair, false dream.

He'll not spare your rivers! their bosom must part
   To the keel, and the wheel of the noisy mill;
   They'll be spanned by bridges, and dammed until
A sudden pain is felt in your heart,
And you turn from the scene of this murderous Art—
   But what can you do? 'Tis your master's will!

Your plains will be crushed by the ponderous weight
   Of the structures and wonders he'll plan and build!
   Your sun-clad vales will be torn and tilled,
Should you with this wrinkled lover mate;
Nor would all that you have his craving sate,
   Till the last of your herds is driven and killed!

And temples he'll rear on your honest wold;
   And above their doors will Justice stand,
   With her balanced scales in her stainless hand;
While Injustice within shall his scales uphold,
Which yield to the weight of the perjuring gold,
   That triumphs o'er Justice in all his land!

Your moon and stars will be shadowed and crossed
   By a net-work of wire, that shall bridge the air!
   And lights will flash with a frightful glare—
As the funeral pyre of the world you have lost!
And you on a rack, shall be tortured and tossed,
   As you meet the gaze of its skeleton stare.

Your cottonwood groves neath the axe will fall!
   Your roses and blossoms will meet the flame!
   And you, with a face that is dyed with shame,
Will shrink too late—*for he will have all*—
From the touch of the dreaded death-like pall,
   That folds you for aye, and wreathes him with fame.

Those monarchs, your fathers, who came to your side,
   Through danger and darkness so long ago,
   Will bow their heads in uttermost woe,
Should they see you robed as the cold East's bride!
And they'd seek them a home on the sea's broad tide;—
   And by bidding him come, you bid them go.

Those comrades of mine who still with you stay,
   Will scabbard their sabres, and loose their steeds!
   Would you give those friends, for the swaying reeds,
That lean to you now with each coming day?
As the new advances, the old recedes!
   Do you feel you can part with *them* this way?

Would you sell your birth-right, my noble West,
   For a love that is born of a base desire?
   Would you bring destruction and death and ire
To those who have loved you longest and best?
I tell you the love that the East confessed
   Will blacken your soul like a satan-sent fire!

But love was never nor shall be swayed!
    'Tis the strongest passion that rules the breast;
    And if you are doomed for his bride, my West,
The bitterest debt of my life is paid!
Tho' I'll cherish you still as the comeliest maid,
    That ever by nature wild, was dressed.

And down in my heart I will rear me a shrine,
    To the pure wild maid I have loved so long;
    And I'll bring to its altar my tears and song—
My passionate tears, and my doubtful rhyme!
And in fancy at least I will dwell in the clime,
    Whose air I breathed, till my star set wrong!

CLEOPATRA'S PROTEST.

Come nearer my spotted leopard, and cool with your
    tongue my hand,
I am faint with a fitful fever, and filled with a fancy
    grand,
Lie close to my side, and lend me your passion that
    poison taints,
While I ponder the perjured picture the world of your
    mistress paints;
The features and life it has painted, and chiseled and
    moulded and sung,
Of Egypt's Cleopatra in every land and tongue;
On canvas, crystal, china, in bronze and brass and
    gold;
In malachite and marble, on coins and medals old
In mosaic and murrhine, in coral, copper, clay;
On ivory and in ebon, in Scotia's granite grey;
In opal, ophite, onyx, in sapphire, chrysolite;
In topaz, turquoise, jasper; in alabaster white;
In verse and prose and ballad, in history manifold,
The face and life of Egypt's queen is drawn and carved
    and told.
In this galaxy of artists, in this gallery of art,
Where chisel, brush and pen have vied to do their
    perjured part,

I see no shade nor shadow, no sign nor semblance see,
Of her who stood at Actium with Roman Antony!
I fail to find the features, the force or spirit bold,
Of her who sailed the Cydnus in her galley wrought in gold;
In the character they give me I trace no sign nor mood
Of hers, who chose destruction to a life of servitude;
Who bared her bosom proudly and perished like a Queen,
Preferring death to Cæsar, and the grave to Roman spleen!
But I see the spiteful venom that guided steel and hand,
That tarnished as it tinted, and poisoned as it planned.
I see the jealous envy that shaped each curve and turn,
Of chisel, brush and pencil; but naught of truth discern;
And I see what they have made me, I cannot help but see,
For what the senseless store omits, is found in history.
The seal they set upon me of sumptuous sin and shame,
They stole from frail Aspasia's brow, and Grecian Phryne's name.
I see the perjured picture! I see the wanton vile,
They show for Cleopatra—"the Serpent of the Nile;"
And the eager world in earnest the counterfeit accepts,
And down through coming ages the truthful type rejects;
But I scorn to see the semblance in the picture that they draw,
Of her who held Rome captive, and whose wish was Egypt's law!
I would bid them go remember that she whom they revile,

Spurned the love of laureled Cæsar, when he sought her
   by the Nile
And offered fame and station, and the sovereignty of
   Rome,
If she would yield the conquest, and say she was his
   own!
That she sent him back, with others, in their regal
   robes unmanned,
Who had come as hopeful suitors for Cleopatra's hand,
And bid them lay their treasures at the feet of one
   more free,
Than the spouse of Rome's Triumvir—the God-like
   Antony!
I would tell them that the pious prude, Octavia, whom
   they raise
Upon the highest pinnacle of purity and praise,
Is not worthy of the worship they offer at her shrine,
For she was never Antony's; he always had been mine!
He took her from her regal home to carry out his part,
But never to his bosom, and never to his heart;
And all, all, all of Antony this haughty dame can
   claim,
Is the sacrifice he offered when he gave to her his name!
He has sworn to me by Eros, beneath the Libyan
   moon,
That he never held her nearer than that peerless
   plenilune;
He has sworn it o'er and over that their hands have
   never met,
And that his star in Egypt rose, when her's in Rome
   had set!

I would tell them that Octavia knew his spirit and his heart,
His life, his soul, his destiny, his mind, his every part
Was moored upon the Nilus, together with mine own,
Before he ever sought her—by Cæsar's wish alone.
And she knew the god's of Egypt had smiled serenely down
On the union of Rome's consul, with Egypt's starry crown!
I would tell them she they blemished with the brand of sin and shame,
Would have scorned to call him husband who gave alone his name!
And had that haughty Roman dame the spirit of a dove,
She'd have sent him back to Egypt, to her who owned his love.

I am weary; leave me leopard! you cannot change your skin,
Nor I the haughty spirit I showed to all save him.
And I thank the gods of Egypt for their mercy, which was shone
In giving me Mark Antony for all, all, all mine own!
And I thank the god of waters for yielding me the tide,
That flooded old Nile's bosom, where we rode side by side;
And to those who called me "Sorceress," and "Serpent of the Nile,"
And to those who dubbed me "Tigress," and every thing that's vile,

CLEOPATRA'S PROTEST.

I would say, your shafts fell harmless, for we were
    wholly one,
And when the pulse of one did cease, the other's life
    had run.
So I banish bitter feelings for all who did malign,
For 'twas but human nature to envy bliss like mine;
And I rain forgiveness on them in pearly perfumed
    showers;
And tell them that the western world knew naught of
    love like ours.

A PROPHECY.

Down the meadow one day in the morning of May,
    Tripped a maiden both tender and fair;
The sun in its joy with her features did toy,
    And played with her amber gold hair:
He gamboled in glee on her lips which were free
    From the pressure of covetous man,
And his scintillant streak o'er her rose-tinted cheek,
    In freedom and ecstasy ran.

The maiden soon stooped where some daisies were grouped,
    And gathered the best from the fold,
And unto them said, "Tell me which I shall wed,
    Whether beauty, or station or gold?"
She repeated them slow, as the petals like snow
    Wavered airily down to their bed;
But the prophet soon spoke, and the last that she broke
    Proclaimed it was GOLD she would wed.

Three times then essayed the credulous maid
    To alter the fortune foretold;
But the prophet maintained that it could not be changed,
    And thrice reasserted 'twas "GOLD!"
Then she questioned if Fate had decreed she must wait
    A day, or a month or a year,
Ere her lover confessed that 'twas she he loved best,
    And he sought her with feelings sincere;

A PROPHECY.

Then the petals so white in their wavering flight,
    Fell again to their soft tufted bed,
And the daisy once more told the fortune in store,
    And "day" was the word that it said.
Then she said, "Fairy dear, little wizard I fear
    The future you falsely relate;
For though you say "day" in your positive way,
    I know it is years I must wait."

Down the meadow one day in the morning of May,
    Strolled a guardsman of elegant mien,
His figure and face both betokened his race,
    And his features were haughty and keen:
On History's fold was his valor enrolled,
    Recounting brave deeds he had done!
And the name which he bore, down through ages of yore,
    Was as pure and unstained as the sun.

The soldier soon stooped where some daisies were grouped,
    And gathered the best from the fold,
And unto them said, "Tell me which I shall wed,
    Whether beauty, or culture or gold?"
The petals so white in their wavering flight,
    Fell airily down to their bed;
But the prophet soon spoke, and the last that he broke
    Proclaimed it was "GOLD!" he would wed.

Then he cried, "Gypsy queen, you, the future have seen
    Through clouds that have shadowed your sight,
For I know years must wane ere my heart can be lain
    At the feet of a maiden so bright!
No, no, little flower! no maid in her bower

Awaits now the sound of my tread;
For my heart is as cold as the stone which was rolled
  To its tomb in a year that is dead!"

Down the meadow he strolled with his cavalry swing,
  And his lips "Sweetest Eyes" did repeat;
But his song quickly died as the maid he espied,
  With the daisies all strown at her feet.
As he drew near her side her fair cheek was dyed,
  With the color of modesty born,
But it gracefully fled when their greetings were said,
  And they spoke of the glorious morn.

. . . . . .

Then he told her, her face was the same he had seen
  At his side, when of Heaven he dreamed;
That her eyes were as bright as the meteor light,
  Which forth from that vision had gleamed;
That the lark's silvery tone was less sweet than her own;
  That her form was as perfect and rare
As her dear little mouth, which was warm as the South,
  And as sweet as the blossoms culled there.

He told her a prophet predicted his fate
  Would be met ere the day sunk in night,
And when first they did meet, his heart's rapid beat
  Convinced him the prophet was right;—
That his love was as deep as the billows that leap
  And rush to embrace the warm shore;—
That his heart was as true as the sabre he drew,
  When it won him the honors he wore.

Then he spoke of his race with dignified grace,

A PROPHECY.

And assured her his lineage was pure;
That the gems on his breast were a nation's bequest,
And he felt not unworthy to woo her;—
That his spurs had been won 'neath an India sun,
When Death held his carnival grim,
And he knew of no stain on his honor or name,
That the future's fair prospect could dim.

Then he told her his heart of herself was a part,
And 'twas hers that he hoped to obtain;
And he said, "Little dear, should you doubt I'm sincere,
The words of my prophet prove vain;
And the rest of my life will be one endless strife
In pursuit of contentment and rest,
For my heart ever true will still cling unto you,
And refuse to be torn from your breast."

The voice of the maid slight emotion betrayed
As she answered, "I too had a dream,
And yours is the face which that vision did grace,
And made it a Paradise seem;
Your hand is the same in which mine was then lain,
And I'm sure you are noble and true,
For all I held bright in my ideal knight,
I behold now embodied in you."

She told him a fairy had whispered her heart
Would be won ere the sun sank from view,
And though lightly she dwelt on the presage, she felt
The words of her prophet were true;
For she knew that the thrill which her being did fill,
Was the prelude to Love's golden chime;

And she knew the heart-beat, in her breast did repeat
    The strain of his own ringing rhyme.

She told him she came of a race that held fame
    And honor as needful as breath,
And that all of her line were as true as the vine
    That closely will cling, e'en in death.
She said that her past by no cloud was o'er cast;
    That her life was as pure as the air;—
That her heart was as free as the fetterless sea,
    Till he came as its conqueror there.

Then she turned to his face with exquisite grace,
    And said, "Now my dream is fulfilled,
For the Paradise seen in the flights of a dream,
    Is the future that Destiny willed!
And besides, could I choose this bright future to lose,
    The fortune our prophets fore-told,
Would convince me that Fate had decreed for each mate
    The heart that the other would hold."

Then they laughed at the dower, which their wizard the flower
    Had told them they surely would wed;
For neither had gold, and their love had been told,
    And the whispers that pledged them were said.
They felt that no power could darken the hour
    They looked to with pleasure and pride,
And the future should prove the great strength of their love,
    Which would flow with unchangeable tide.

    .   .   .   .   .   .

Two years have passed by since the guardsman drew nigh
    To that maid of the meadow, in May;
Tho' she still may be seen on its cushion of green,

A PROPHECY.

With a daisy to which she doth say:
"*Il m'aime, un peu, passionnément, beaucoup;*
  O *marguerite,* I pray you say not *point du tout!*"
And the *marguerite* obeyed the sweet voice of the maid,
  And the petal remaining, but "*passionnément*" said.

. . . .

In a land far removed from the one that he loved,
  The guardsman is calling to day
On the daisies, to learn if the maid doth return
  The love which he gave her in May.
"*Elle m'aime, un peu, passionnément, beaucoup,*"
  He says, "O my *marguerite,* say not *point du tout!*"
And the flower ever true kept his wishes in view,
  And the petal that lingered said "*passionnément*" too.

. . . .

Another year dawns, and the maiden now mourns
  The loss of her lover so dear;
The cruel news came that her hero was slain
  While striving the colors to rear.
That was all that it said, and the heart-striken maid
  Murmured not at Fate's merciless tread;
Tho' she knew that her life on that field of red strife,
  By the side of her lover lay dead.

. . . . . .

Years pass as they bring tender blossoms of Spring,
  And Winter's cold shrouding of snow;
And the maiden is wed by her father's death bed,
  While her heart is still numb in its woe.
She is wedded with "GOLD" as the daisy foretold!
  But her heart and her hopes lie entombed

In that far foreign land where he fell with his band,
    When her future forever was doomed.

    .   .   .   .   .   .

The war now is o'er, and from shore unto shore
    Rings the echoing chorus of peace :
The guardsman, with those who were held by their foes,
    Receives his long looked-for release.
All the suffering and fears he had borne the long years
    He was held in the enemy's power,
Seemed a dream of the past, which with joy was o'er cast
    As he felt the approach of the hour.

Let us lower a veil o'er his grief, when the tale
    That the maiden was wed reached his ears;
Let us banish from view the torture she knew,
    When they met after all those long years.
She told him her heart in that strife took a part,
    Till dead by his side it was lain ;
And the vows which she said by her father's death bed,
    Were spoken to lighten his pain :

That she never had known aught of love, save his own,
    That her heart to his life she did yield ;
And that now when too late, by the weaving of Fate,
    It comes with the dead from that field ;
That its passion so old could now never be told,
    For God's law like a conquering sea,
Reaches out to enfold the sands where once rolled
    Their river of Love, deep and free.

He told her he knew that her heart had been true,
    That Fate had their destiny sealed ;

A PROPHECY.

And he would that the foe who that day laid him low,
    Had ended his life on that field. .
So they parted in tears, that had smothered for years
    The flood of their passionate tide,
And the pulse in each breast all the anguish expressed,
    Their dumb trembling lips sought to hide.

Years blossom and wane ere the lovers again
    To that meadow together repair;
But they sought it with pride, for she went as his bride,
    After cycles of sorrow and care:
She had brought him the "GOLD" that the daisies fore-told,
    With the heart that had ever been true;
And the ecstasy seen in the flights of a dream.
    After anguish and torture they knew.

.   .   .   .   .   .

A grave now is seen in that meadow so green.
    And the slab leaning low by its side,
Shows that death could not part the soldier's warm heart
    From the life of his long cherished bride:
And the daisies that bloom on their blossoming tomb
    Tell the lovers and maids of to-day
The workings of Fate, but they scorn till too late
    To heed what the prophets do say.

AN EPISODE.

Where the brook like a bridge spans the highway,
    Where the willow and locust lean low,
Where the vines form an arch to a by-way
    O'er shadowed with clumped mistletoe,
And the air with fresh perfume is laden,
        They met long ago;
        And the sun sinking slow
        Shed its scintillant glow
    On the face of a man and a maiden,
        Who met by that brook long ago.

They met all unknown and unbidden,
    And paused in the brook side by side,
But their eyes were cast downward and hidden,
    As their horses bent low to the tide
And uttered a monotone neigh :
        Then the circles ebbed wide,
        Rippling on in their pride,
        Babbling on to confide
    The love that they bore in their way ;
        While the maiden and man watched the tide.

AN EPISODE.

Side by side, though a world rose between them
   They sat, and a stillness profound
Stole down with the sunlight to screen them,
   Stole down with the gloaming around;
Yet still to the ripples they listed:
      Then her hair came unbound,
      And it slowly unwound
      From its coil golden crowned;
   From its coil that was braided and twisted,
      From its coil that with beauty was crowned.

His glance for an instant detected
   Her face through that lattice of hair;
His glance for an instant inspected
   The modest confusion flushed there;
Then the maid he addresses:
      "O maiden so fair!
      O maiden so rare!
      O golden brown hair!
   You have woven my heart in your tresses,
      O would 'twere forever bound there!"

Had she heard? Was that side glance a token
   Responsive to love he had told?
Then why not have lingered and spoken?
   Why leave him so cruelly cold?
Why leave him this pitiful guerdon?
      "O story so old!
      O lover so bold!
      O world stern and cold!
   I dare not my poor heart unburden,
      I dare not its secret unfold!"

What was it she shrouded in sable?
  What secret she dreaded to tell?
What story, Love's anguishing fable?
  What vision feared she to dispel?
What spectre had caused her to start?
    Who can say? Who can tell?
    Who can say if the bell
     Pealed a chime, tolled a knell,
  As it rang in the tower of her heart,
    Who can say, rang it wildly or well?

And he, what strange spirit inspired him
  To utter that passionate prayer?
Had her beauty, so marvellous, fired him
  With courage disdaining despair?
Did her eyes speak her soul?
    Did the wealth of her hair,
    And her modesty rare
    Bespeak her so fair,
    Bespeak her so perfect a whole—
    Or temptingly said they "BEWARE?"

Who shall say? we cannot who come after,
  Nor can they who are long gone before;
Sad thought, but grief quails before laughter!
  Let us banish the thought evermore;
Let us fly as she fled from disaster,
    Striving not to explore,
    Lest we praise and adore,
    Lest we beg and implore;
    O Love thou unconquerable master!
    We fear thee, yet seek and adore.

AN EPISODE.

So they met in the brook and so parted:
   As strangers they met all unknown;
As lovers they left, broken-hearted,
   As lovers from Love they had flown,
And divided they nurtured their sorrow,
     Divided they stilled their heart's moan;
     His—"Alone! all alone!"
     Hers—"Atone? I atone!
   But too late, there could dawn no to-morrow!
   There could brighten no happier zone.

A grave rears its mound 'neath the willow
   That bends to the brook's babbling tide;
A grave spreads its dank, mossy pillow
   'Neath the locust that leans at its side;
Thither led by a ghost, I repair;
     With a ghost for a guide,
     With a ghost for a bride,
     With a ghost of a love at my side!
   And I muse, lies she there with the golden
     brown hair?
   Lies he there, who sat here by her side?

IN MEMORIAM.

[*Colonel Geo. A. Gordon, U. S. A. Died Nov. 26th, 1878.*]

Why is it the arms of the Fifth to-day bear
    A badge that is sombre in hue?
Why is it the hilts of its sabres so fair
    Are shrouded with crape from our view?
Why falls the old flag from its eminence high,
    And droops at the half mast so still?
Why shrieks the old eagle with pitiful cry
    As he soars o'er the Western hill?

Oh! does not yon riderless steed draped in black,
    Hung in housing of sable and gloom,
And the old dragoon boots, hanging empty and slack
    From the saddle where Death has made room,
Denote that a chieftain his station has changed,
    And moved in advance of his band,
To those fields where the seraphs in glory are ranged,
    To welcome him home to their land?

The Fifth's veteran roster to-day shows a blank
    Which the loved name of Gordon long filled;
And the glittering leaves—those bright emblems of rank,
    Lie withered and faded and chilled.
The flag 'neath whose folds his bright laurels were won
    Is now draping his motionless form,
For the Fifth's truest hero and noblest son,
    Was mustered in Heaven this morn.

Never more will the reveille bugle awake
    Its hero at dawning of day,
Never more on his ear will the sweet music break
    Of his steed's old familiar neigh;
Never more will the "charge" light with pleasure his face
    As of old in the days that are gone;
He has answered the "recall" with soldier-like grace,
    Which from Heaven was plaintively borne.

Once again must the Fifth place another loved name
    On that tablet to Memory reared,
Where the names of her sons shine in glorious fame,
    When from roster and roll they are cleared ;
So, high where the names of "Bache," "Crittenden,"
        "Brown,"
"Burns," "Almy," and "Rodgers" are seen,
She must place that of Gordon beneath her proud crown,
    And see that 'tis ever kept green.

CUSTER'S FUNERAL.

Genl. Geo. A. Custer, U. S. A. Killed at the battle of the Little Big Horn, Mon. Ter. June 25th, 1876. Re-interred at West Point, N. Y. Oct. 1877

With arms reversed,
Solemnly, solemnly tread!
Column move mournfully
   Home with your dead!
Autumn lends leaves of red,
Heaven her tears has shed,
Softening your solemn tread
   Down to the grave.

"Rest on Arms!"
Silently, silently bow;
God's is the service
   You're serving in now.
Crushed is the Army's pride,
Craped are her colors wide,
Palled is her heart beside
   The coffined brave.

Load and Fire!
"Steadily, steadily men!"
Such was the caution
   He gave to you, when

Far on Montana's plain,
Seeing all hope was vain,
Charging through leaden rain,
  Boldly he led !

Lower him down tenderly,
Tenderly lower ;
Gaze on your color-draped
  Chieftain once more.
Hide not that tear-dimmed eye,
Hush not that sobbing sigh ;
Did not a Nation cry
  "CUSTER IS DEAD !"

Sound the "Taps" mournfully,
Mournfully sound :
Disturb not the sleepers
  Encamped on this ground ;
Here where a youth he staid,
Here where the man was made,
Here is the warrior laid
  Wreathed in his fame.

Hudson roll onward,
Roll rapidly on !
Bear on thy bosom
  This burden of song—
Custer, thy name shall be
Honored in history !
Valor and bravery,
Down to posterity
  Cling to thy name !

A VICTIM OF FATE.

I was drifted last night by the driving snow
    To the glimmering sheen of a window bright;
The laces drooped, and the curtains were low,
    But the light flashed out on the dismal night.
The strain of a soul-stirring waltz of Strauss
    Was borne to my ears on the wavering snow,
As I pressed my form to the sheltering house,
    And mused on the Fate that had wrought my woe.

And above my thoughts I seemed to hear
    The shimmering slide of the satiny feet,
As they moved in time to the music clear,
    And chimed with the rhythm their glad hearts beat;
And the whispered word, and the low reply
    That was breathed in the tiny jeweled ear—
The smothered response, and the stifled sigh,
    And the silvery laugh—all seemed so near.

My sensitive soul 'neath the weather-worn coat
    That hung to my wasted and shivering form,
Again on the bosom of bliss did float,
    Beyond the scope of the pitiless storm;
I felt the sweep of a silken dress,
    And the rose-leaf touch of a tender hand;
I toyed once more with an amber tress,
    That was coiled with a blossom and golden band.

A VICTIM OF FATE.

I gazed in the eyes, where Love enthroned
   On the mirrored soul his kingdom held—
The eyes I had cherished, and loved and owned,
   Ere conquering Fate had my life-tree felled!
I felt the perfumed breath as it stole
   So warm o'er my beaten and frosted face;
I felt the thrill in my hopeless soul
   Of the nectared kiss, and the fond embrace.

I lived again in the buried Past—
   The Past on whose grave the flowers yet bloom;
Few Winters can boast that their chilling blast
   Has beat at the door of its desolate tomb:
I lived again in that Past so dead,
   When the very doors where I then leaned cold,
Were opened wide to my welcomed tread,
   As my liveried brougham o'er the pavement rolled.

The petted, privileged, idolized beau
   Of Fashion's queens, in her gilded halls,
Now beats from his breast the driving snow,
   And begs his bread at the market stalls.
Yes, I who leaned by the portal rods
   Where beauty and fashion and wealth were clanned,
Once held the power of those worshiped gods
   In the hollow palm of this bony hand!

Ah, Retrospect! thou art Satan's tool,
   Coached by thy master his cause to win;
Thy pupils are trained in a tinseled school,
   And graduate in the temple of Sin!
I see the fire on thy altar bright,
   Where greater and purer than I have kneeled;

But I'll bow at the shrine long dead to light,
   Where Honor deserted, its life did yield.

Yes, I the penniless, shelterless tramp,
   With a desolate heart and a burdened soul,
Will turn from the flame of thy baneful lamp
   Which would lure me on to its tempting goal!
Forgotten by God, and to man obscure,
   Loathed by woman, and shunned by maid,
I'll cling to my honor unsullied and pure,
   Till the heart's throbs cease, and the life doth fade!

I hear your mocking, incredulous tone
   As you say: "Presumptuous! how very droll!
Doubtless a villian from justice flown;
   What nonsense! 'honor,' and 'heart' and 'soul'!"
But I tell you since Adam by God was planned,
   Since the world was soiled by Satan's breath,
Honor and poverty, hand in hand,
   Together have marched to the doors of death!

Honor and poverty, hunger and truth,
   Hand in hand, with reverent tread,
A-down through ages unknown to ruth,
   Have crossed the chasm where sleep the dead.
You may scoff till the earth its course has run,
   You may cite "Statistics," and "Pauper Acts;"
But all the arguments under the sun
   Will fail to alter the pitiful facts!

Ay! pitiful, merciless, shameful facts,
   That will blot forever the Christian page,
While Poverty's print and Crime's base acts
   Are reckoned akin by the hoary sage!

A VICTIM OF FATE.

The matron of Charity's homes and wards,
   In racking torture is equally learned
With the warder grim, who the culprit guards,
   Where the window is barred and the key is turned.

And I, whose life is as free from crime,
   Dishonor, falsehood, deceit and spleen,
As the lark's who carols his matin chime,
   Am stamped by the world, "*Unclean !*" "*Unclean !*"
(*I*, who by coaxing my conscience to sleep,
   By bidding my honor one jot to yield,
Might the golden grains of the harvest reap
   That I left for dead in a blighted field!)

But I heed it not, and forever I'll stand
   A Victim of Fate, till my pulse is stilled !
Though bony and cold, mine's an honest hand,
   And would scorn the purse that dishonor filled!
Though tattered and torn are the garments I wear,
   Heavy both heart and soul with pain,
A plentiful past—and a future bare,
   I would not yield *conscience* the past to gain !

The Past, whose threshold I crossed in youth
   With a guiltless soul, and a trustful heart,
Believing that Honor, Virtue and Truth
   Were the staple goods of the worldly mart ;
Believing that Honor, Virtue and Truth,
   Were the beacons that burned in the wake of Fame,
Believing—as taught to believe in youth,
   That they were Humanity's pride and aim.

My race was old and my lineage pure,
   My acres broad and my culture fair ;

A VICTIM OF FATE.

The future, in fancy seemed bright and sure,
   And the past was unclouded by sorrow or care.
While youth was yet in its chrysalis state,
   Awaiting its second birth as man,
I passed through the glittering golden gate
   Where the river of fashion and splendor ran.

On the billowy breast of that fragrant flood
   A bubble I floated to Pleasure's sea,
Where a god I arose, and sun-crowned stood,
   And the river was hushed in idolatry.
I was worshiped and praised by that passionate tide
   Which bore its pearls to my gilded shrine,
And every ebb of its current so wide
   Was guided and governed by will of mine.

I was copied and quoted, toasted and sung,
   By lord and lady, by great and learned!
And over me ever a censer swung,
   Where the perfume of Power like incense burned.
I learned each pulse of that feverish stream,
   The throb of each heart which its bosom veiled;
I traversed the course of its fair, false gleam
   To the great dark sea, where its current paled.

Did I find what my fancy had pictured there—
   Honor and Virtue stainless and pure?
Did I find the real, as the ideal fair—
   Barred from the contact of vice secure?
I found but a babbling, glittering stream
   Flowing madly on in its fierce desire,
Beneath whose bosom, beyond the gleam,
   Lay the serpent's slime and the poisonous mire!

I found that truth and conscience were naught,
    If they barred the passage that led to Fame !
That honor and virtue were sold and bought
    For an idle whim, as a passing game !
That the crime of sin was a burden light,
    Which was borne on its bosom in babbling song ;
That detection in sin was a withering blight—
    And that in *detection* lay all the wrong !

I followed its course from its fountain birth
    To its tomb where it sinks in the surging sea ;
Its reaching branches which spanned the earth
    From land to land, were known to me.
Its flow in the North 'neath its bosom of ice,
    Its Southern course with its sun-kissed breast,
Was over the same veiled sloughs of vice
    That lay 'neath its tides from East to West.

I had drunk of the life of that treacherous stream,
    I had bathed in its azureline fitful flood,
Ere I woke to life from the mocking dream,
    And found 'twas the Styx where a god I stood.
I stepped from my throne with its gilded shrine,
    I washed from my garments and soul each stain
Of that fulsome stream, whose poisonous slime
    Should never defile my life again !

'Twas a dreary dawn I was destined to see,
    With threatening clouds that gloomily hung
O'er the dreams that had pictured life to me,
    Ere that subtle stream had their requiem sung.
My life seemed wrecked, and my purpose gone ;
    My friends seemed false, and the world impure ;

A VICTIM OF FATE.

My soul was shamed, and my hopes forlorn,
    For triumphing Sin did success insure!

The struggle was great, but at length I awoke
    From the chaos of gloom that enveloped my life;
I freed myself from its burdensome yoke,
    And laid the siege to a fruitless strife.
I labored and lectured, I wrote and read.
    I lavished my fortune and wearied my brain;
I preached and practised, I counseled and plead
    In Honor's cause, against Satan's reign.

The siege was just, and the conflict long!
    But Fate compelled me perforce to yield,
And with health and fortune forever gone,
    Deserted I stood on a vanquished field.
My effort was vain! for my purpose grand
    No impression left, not a vestige more
Than the curlew leaves in the shifting sand
    That is washed by the waves on a barren shore!

The stream flowed on with its breast laid bare,
    Which temptingly swelled 'neath the sun's warm light,
And thousands thronged to its banks so fair,
    Who longed to be borne on its bosom bright.
Nor a bubble was swayed, nor a ripple was turned
    By my labor of years, which no harvest did yield;
On the altar of Satan its fire still burned,
    Where woman and maiden and manhood kneeled.

Yes; thousands on thousands that fair stream sought,
    And strove to dip in its current so grand;
While I, who with hunger and poverty fought,
    Would wash its trace from my friendless hand!

And I who once was its chosen god,
  Ere I fathomed the depths where its soul was hid,
Would bear the scourge of the tyrant's rod,
  Could I bury *that* thought 'neath the coffin lid !

I would lengthen this life of hunger and pain
  Without complaint, to the end of time,
Could I banish that thought from my weary brain,
  Which maddens my soul like poisonous wine !
Could I but forget that the goddess of Grace
  Who now sweeps by with a glance of scorn,
Has pillowed her cheek on this furrowed face,
  And fretfully wept at the severing dawn.

But it must not be ; for with every breath
  Come zephyrs that waft me against my will !
They sway my helm from the port of Death,
  And quicken the pulse I strive to still.
But perhaps with the light of the Judgment morn,
  When God is the Justice who reigns supreme,
This Victim of Fate, now a creature forlorn,
  May appear to His vision not quite "Unclean."

'TWAS *AU REVOIR*.

Her hand was in his as they stood by the gate
   'Neath the light of the mellow moon,
And their thoughts were absorbed by the pitiless fate
   That severed their lives so soon :
'Twas a pleading, passionate face that he saw
   As her lips to his own he drew,
And sighed, "Let it, darling, be *au revoir*,
   But never till death, *adieu*."

Heart beat against heart as they silently stood,
   And the mellow moon hung above ;
But their lips could not speak what their spirits would
   Tho' their eyes beamed with languor and love.
Then her hand from his clasp she did tenderly draw,
   And her arms round his neck she threw,
As she sobbed, "Yes, my darling, 'tis *au revoir*,
   But never till death, *adieu*."

Lip clung to lip as they stammered and swayed,
    While the moon with a vapory cloud
Veiled its face from the anguish the scene portrayed,
    And wept 'neath its misty shroud.
So they hopefully parted ; and he to the war
    Sped onward, its horrors to view,
His lips still repeating, "'Twas *au revoir !*"
    And hers, "Not till death *adieu.*"

Again by the lichened gate she stands,
    And her pale face seeks the moon,
As she raises to Heaven her suppliant hands,
    And sobs, "Ah ! 'twas selfishly soon."
And tho' with fresh laurels he came from the war,
    The flag hid his form from her view ;
And the stone where they lie bears, "'TWAS AU REVOIR,"
    And—"NOT EVEN IN DEATH ADIEU."

JEANETTE'S (HYPOTHETICAL) ANSWER.

I have loosened the snood that I wear, my love,
As I'd loosen the stars in the skies above,
If 'twould bring to my darling one hour's delight,
Or banish the day and hasten the night,
That is filled with sweet thoughts of my love, my love!

I know that my eyes tell the tale, my love,
And the pulse of my heart doth its ardor prove!
But how can I screen what my soul lays bare—
What flows in my blood, and gleams in my hair,
When I feel the warm touch of thy hand, my love?

My lips, which thou sayest are fresh, my love,
As the twitter of birds, and the coo of the dove,
Are filled with the nectar they drunk in thine,
Which filled me and thrilled me like olden wine,
As I quaffed the rich sweets of thy lips, my love!

JEANETTE'S ANSWER.

If I've tangled thy life in my hair, my love,
May Cupid lean down from his Eden above,
And weave them so closely they never shall part—
Thy life with my tresses, my heart with thy heart,
That we're one till the end of time, my love.

Ah! do not speak so of thine arms, my love!
For they circle my world and my heaven above;
And when lovingly clasped round thine own little "Pet"
All the sorrows and cares of my life I forget;
And I'd nestle for aye in those arms, my love!

So mourn nevermore for thy "Pet," my love,
For she's ever thine own Jeanette, my love!
And all that thou holdest so sweet and so fair—
Her "grey swimming eyes," and her lips and her hair,
Are thine to the grave and beyond, my love!

ALONE AT THE SPRINGS.

Alone at the Springs! All alone at the Springs!
    What a harvest of gloom such retrospect brings
To those who were there ere the summer did wane,
    When the courted queen Fashion triumphant did reign:
When the parlors and porches were thronged with her clan,
    And the river of Pleasure in ecstasy ran ;
When the rustic retreats and each vine-trellised grove,
    Were filled with the incense and whispers of love.

It would seem to them drear, as it does to the one
    Who lingers behind when the season is done ;
And with senses unsealed to the weirdness and gloom
    Wanders aimlessly on through each vacant old room.
To the ball-room, where oft he hath turned to the strain
    Of the sweetest of Strauss', his steps tend again ;
And the parlors he seeks, but there lingers no tone
    Of the voice or the ballad she said was his own.

With a copy of Story he strolls to the springs,
    But the poem is lost in the thoughts that it brings ;
For his mind, 'gainst his will, strays again to the one
    Who sat with him there when the summer was young.

He leans 'gainst the tree where he cut her dear name,
    But even the sturdy old oak's not the same ;
Its vestment of verdure no longer is worn,
    The sereness of Autumn has Summer's garb shorn.

He broods in his loneness on days that are fled,
    And gathers this spoil from the field of the dead ;—
A head of rare beauty with exquisite grace
    Lightly throned on his shoulder, and raising a face
More dazzling and perfect than ever was seen
    When angels of Paradise brightened the dream ;
With love-swimming eyes melting sweetly to his,
    And dewy red lips slightly cleft for his kiss.

An arm—nor less fair than the soft snowy lawn
    That in delicate folds o'er her bosom was drawn—
Encircling his neck, while a hand soft and fair,
    With a lily-like touch from his brow smooths the hair:
A smothered, "You love me?" a stifled, "As true
    As the stars that are fixed in the firmament blue !"
A mingling of lips—a delectable thrill,
    And the death harvest's gathered ; the reaper is still.

O why should one summon these wraiths from their tomb?
    Have they power to dispel the oppression of gloom!
Is it pleasure or anguish, or comfort or pain,
    That beats in our breast as they rise up again ?
Is it nectar we sip, or Dead Sea fruit we taste,
    As we muse on the bounty, and witness the waste ?
Is it ecstasy's thrill, or despair's bitter pang,
    The sweets of the rose, or the snake's venomed fang,

ALONE AT THE SPRINGS.

That tingles our veins when the reverie's gone,
   And we wake to encounter the present, forlorn?
'Tis the triumph of torture! the glory of grief!
   The demon of anguish, that comes like a thief,
Stealing all of the Past that is blissful and dear,
   And leaving to us but the palsied and sere!
'Tis the stern god of sorrow, depriving of peace
   The poor wearied soul that but seeks its surcease!

Then why doth he pause on this grave of the Past?
   Why cling to the spot where their lips met the last?
Why in fancy live over the blisses so dead,
   When the light that he seeks nevermore can be shed?
Because, should he part from the scenes of old days—
   Which he feels in a measure yet breathe of her ways,
It would seem unto him as if *he* cleft in twain,
   The tie which he fancies may bind them again.

JIM LEE.

So yer want to see my papers, and hear my right to the claim
Of the mine that's known as "Lydia," and yer want to learn my name?
Well, picket yerselves round the embers, and listen to what I tell,
And yer'll find my claim to the "Lydia's," as good as the Devil's to Hell!
'Twas back in the States in '50 that my heart began to buck,
And as curb and spur wouldn't answer, I thought as I'd try my luck;
So I slipped to her ranch, and told her that I loved her with all my sand,
And that I'd go blind with this heart here, if she'd chip along with her hand.
We played the game "pat," and then quitted; I came out a little ahead,
Then started to find her Guv'ner, to tell him his girl I'd wed.
Yer may have seen short-horns in Texas, and bronchos in Angeles bred,

But strangers the first class in bucking, had always
    Lyd's guv. at the head!
He rared, and screamed and snorted, and asked me
    the weight of my dust;
And when I told him "prospecting," he freshened
    again and cussed;
But those days in the States were quiet like, men
    didn't resort to the "drop,"
So the guv'ner shuffled the pasteboards, and dealt
    them square from the top.
He told me when five Decembers had into five
    Aprils rolled,
I again could come to his dwelling, and lay at his
    feet my gold;
And that if the heap should suit him, and Lyd.
    hadn't changed her mind,
He'd see if he then could swallow the thought of
    our getting jined.
I felt kind o' side-lined and hobbled as I read unto
    Lydia the law,
And showed her the hand he had dealt me, to "*fill*"
    in a five card draw;
But Lyd.—flood that cup there, stranger, that name
    kind o' chokes me now;
But I'm always saying it over, and over and over,
    "How!"
Well, Lyd. she tumbled the sentence over a bit in
    her mind,
Then she promised to wait till her hair was gray,
    or till I my stake should find;
So we—but I reckon I'll skip the parting. 'Tis
    enough if I explain,

JIM LEE.

I saw her kissing her hand to me, 'way back in
    the shady lane.
She had sworn on her heart, and my honor, and
    I on her hand and my life,
That I, only I was her husband, and that she only
    she was my wife.
The "outfit" I had in '50 was a different kind of
    a kit,
From the one you see on my *burro*, but I traded
    it off, and lit
To the mountains just back of "Frisco," and there
    with a pan and a pick,
I started down into the gulches, where I heard
    that the dust was thick.
Yer know what it is in the diggins, yer know how
    yer pan and pan,
And treasure yer dust, and starve yerself, and
    every new comer scan ;
Well, I lived in the mines for nigh two years, and
    was getting a little ahead,
When a letter, it came to me from Lyd., saying
    how the guv. were dead ;
And that how he'd made her promise, beside his
    dying bed,
That she'd stick to the end of the old five years
    before she sought to wed.
That letter it rankled me somewhat, and kind o'
    brought Lyd. to my view,
And seeing her off there alone in the States, it
    made me a trifle blue ;
So I thought if I just could double the pile I had
    stowed away,

I could pack a few pounds of her trouble, and
cheer the girl up for a day:
So I took my dust down to a shanty, and bet my
bag "straight" on the queen;
I'd a "pre" that by backing the woman, I nearer
to Lydia would seem.
Well, she *lost!* and the swallow of whiskey they
handed me back for my pile,
Was all that I had towards helping Lyd., or calm-
ing my rising bile.
Next morning I left for Sonora; this hole in my
arm's all I got!
Then I prospected through Arizona, till Apaches
made panning too hot;
Then I anchored at last on these Hills here, that's
back in July '54,
And I'll chew the fringe of my buckskin shirt if
a white man was here before!
Well, I panned in these hills and gulches, and
took out a power of dust;
But for hash, and sleep and such lux'ries, to my
rifle I had to trust.
I often think now of those old nights, when I in
my dug-out was laid,
A dreaming of bliss I was nearing, till I got kind
o' coward like, and prayed
That my brain might turn off the Sioux bullets, that
my heart might prove stone to their knife,
Till my eyes should again feast on Lydia, and
claim her my own precious wife.
'Twas along in the Spring, I was panning near
the spot where Hill City now stands,

When I saw a thing come down the mountain no
    larger than both of my hands;
But as it came nearer and nearer, I saw 'twas a
    cub of a boy,
So I put down the rifle I'd leveled, lest its mouth
    might his features destroy.
He sprung like a wounded black-tail to my side,
    when I shouted "hullo!"
And clung with his arms to my withers, till I
    thought he would never let go.
Then he told me how he was an orphan, with only
    one friend to his name,
And learning that he was a miner, he out to this
    country had came;
That he'd reckoned on finding his friend here,
    and panning along with him,
But he'd been on the trail for nigh six months,
    and the chances were getting slim.
Then I offered to give him a "shake-down" in the
    dug-out along with me,
And if ever a white boy came to these hills, 'twas
    that same white boy, Jim Lee!
His hands were as small as Lydia's, and as white
    as hers were too,
But I've seen him pan out his pound of dust, and
    knock from his horse the Sioux!
I tell yer, strangers, this Jimmie was a boss from
    the very start,
And could yer have seen him ride and shoot, yer'd
    have rented him out yer heart.
He was Cap. in all professions, and he tidied the
    hut so neat,

JIM LEE.

That often I've stopped on the homeward trail,
    and kicked the clay from my feet.
He was flush with a heap of savey, and of book-
    learning had no end,
And from the moment I spied his phiz, I elected
    myself his friend.
He'd set by the week and listen to the tales I
    would spin him of Lyd.,
And of how I was going home to her, with the
    dust that these gulches hid;
And often I've seen him a-wiping the brine from
    his honest eyes,
As I'd tell him the chances I'd taken, and my
    "pre" that I'd win the prize.
Then he'd tell me how he had staked out his heart
    on another's claim,
But he'd only say, "he's a miner," whenever I
    asked his name;
O if he'd only have given the slip to the name of
    his looked-for pard,
I reckon as how these twenty years would have
    ground by, not so hard!
What with panning, and trapping and yarning,
    the days flew by like mad,
So I laid my plans to scout for home, on the day
    fixed by Lyd's dad;
And I promised to take Jim with me, and if sign
    of his mate w'r'n't seen,
I told him as how that Lydia and I, on the firm
    would allow him a lien.
'Twas just two days to the morning we'd set to
    pull up stakes,

When I found myself hitched in the dug-out with
    a rankling fit of the shakes ;
So Jim just anchored beside me, and we put in
    the time in talk,
Till along towards the shank of evening, when Jim
    started out for a walk.
'Twa'n't more than thirty minutes till I spied Jim
    running back,
And he never broke till he reached my side, and
    dropped at my feet his sack ;
Then he told me how he had located a claim on
    the mountain side,
And had fetched them "croppings" along in his
    bag, to show me the shade of their hide.
Well strangers, them stones Jim brought me would
    have yielded one half to the ton !
Here, fill up that cup again, stranger ; my eyes
    are beginning to run.
Then Jim told me how he had found it, and how
    he'd located his claim,
And how he was staking its boundaries, when I
    thought him hunting for game;
Then he sharpened a stick, and cleared him a
    place on the dug-out floor,
And wrote out a transfer to me of the mine, that
    yielded them croppings of ore.
So *there* is my title, strangers !—but wait, I'm
    ahead of time :
I started right off with Jimmie, and shook all the
    way to the mine ;
Then he showed me the stones he had piled up,
    and a monument bearing my name ;—

Then I saw the bright flash of a rifle, and Jim by
 the monument lain.
Yes, strangers, a Sioux dog had shot him! but I
 sampled his heart to the core,
Ere I turned to my poor little Jimmie to see where
 the bullet had tore :
Well strangers, yer all may be parsons, and I don't
 give a damn if yer be,
I reckon yer'd cussed at yer Maker, if yer'd stood
 in my place by Jim Lee!
I jerked off his little skin jacket, and there on his
 neck was the chain,
And the locket I'd given to Lydia, when I bid
 her good-bye in the lane ;
Yet even then strangers, I tell yer the truth 'from
 my senses was hid,
But a glance at the wound in his heart here, just
 told me that Jimmie—was Lyd !
The rest—hand the cup, is too sacred to retail out
 here as a yarn,
And I tell yer there's only a little left for any of
 you to larn.
Yer *now* know my claim to the "Lydia," the mine
 Jimmie transferred to me ;
And when knocking around to find my name just
 halt when yer reach "Jim Lee."
That's the brand I've carried since '55, and I
 reckon I will not change !
I can always be found at the "Lydia," I've corraled
 it within my range :
The door of my ranch just opens where Jimmie
 had piled his stones,

And the men who have come my claim to dispute,
    have left to my dogs their bones!
Those robes yer see on the ground there, yer took
    for mountain cat,
Are only the scalps of Injuns just trimmed down
    kind o' flat;
I swore by the grave of Lydia I'd settle her claim
    in full,
And those, with a couple more at the ranch, show
    the kind o' trigger I pull.
And all of the gold that's been taken from the
    spot where Lyd. laid her claim,
Is the pile I beat to a kind of a cross, and cut in
    the bar her name;
And it leans just where I put it—by the grave that
    is home to me,
And those who try to disturb it, swap lead with
    old Jim Lee!

I reckon yer think 'tis time my chips were handed
    into the bank;
But I've two things left to live for yet, and nobody
    here to thank:
One is to see that Jimmie's claim to the "Lydia"
    isn't jumped,
And the other's to guard the little mound where
    wild flowers are kind o' clumped!
And strangers, I pack a paper in this locket around
    my neck,
A willing the title to ranch and mine to him who
    shall show respeck

To the carcass of Lee the miner, and plants him
    with his own hands,
Aside of the mound where the flowers are clumped
    where the golden cross still stands:
And the fellow who fills that contract can give
    to his soul a rest,
For if there's a choice in the worlds to come, he's
    certain to pull the best.

CHARITY.

Have you studied that man or that woman?
    Have you learned every phase of their life?
Have you felt each temptation that met them?
    Have you joined in their struggle and strife?
Have you probed every pulse of each bosom?
    Have you measured the throb of each heart?
Have you fathomed their prayers and their passions,
    And the evil from good set apart?

Till you've borne what perhaps they have suffered;
    Till you've found what perchance they have lost;
Till you've seen all of life that is fairest
    With bloodless hands patiently crossed;
Till you've drunk of the chalice, unconscious
    That its lees from deceit are distilled;
Till you've seen every soul you have nurtured
    With crime and corruption instilled,

O refrain from this sitting in judgment
   In causes where all is not known,
And remember Christ said but the stainless
   Shall cast at his brother a stone!
Reflect, ere the cruel word's uttered;
   Desist, ere the action you do;
And ask your own heart in communion,
   If both are not suited to you!

And perchance you may wake to discover
   That the act which in terror you've flown,
Has sown in your own callous bosom
   A virtue it never had known;
And you'll pause, when again you are tempted
   Some merciless tribute to pay,
And ask of your soul's new disciple,
   Wherein am I better than they?

AT THE GRAVE OF C. W. D.

Six moons have lent their lustre to the sod
   That roofs thy resting place—a statesman's tomb;
Six moons have waned since thou to meet thy God,
   Passed from this earth in fullness of thy bloom.

Thy bird-like notes now mid an angel choir
   Doth chant the praises of thy Heavenly King;
Hushed is thine earthly voice and mute the lyre,
   That through long years such happiness did bring.

I kneel upon thy hallowed mound of earth,
   And on my heart, as 'twere a tablet stone,
I write—*Here lies a woman of great worth;*
   It was a gift this woman to have known.

I knew her, loved her, mourn her as a friend—
   The dearest on my rosary of years;
Upon her grave in reverence I bend,
   Nor seek to check my manhood's heart-wrung tears.

AT THE GRAVE OF C. W. D.

A star from out our universe has passed,
   To shine effulgent in a purer sphere;
We see its light—from Heaven's kingdom cast,
   And from its height it sees our sorrow here.

The shadows fall; reluctantly I rise;
   My duty calls me to a land afar:
I raise to Heaven my weary, tear-dimmed eyes,
   And lo, the sheen! it is our missing star.

MARSHFIELD, MASS.
  FEB. 1882.

MEMORIAL VERSES.

ON THE DEATH OF LIEUT. ALFRED B. BACHE, U. S. A.

Another detail has been made from old "F" troop to-day!
Another hero has been called down that mysterous way!
Nor clash of arms, nor ring of steel, nor marshaling of men ;
A grey steed, riderless and houssed, escorts him down the glen.

And close behind, with arms reversed, and slow and measured tread,
The old troop that he loved so well move onward with their dead.
A volley ; "Taps;" and all is o'er ; the orphaned troopers wheel :
Their leader has but gone before : blow bugles ! clash the steel !

Ah, comrades ! little did you think when last you heard him sing
"My Gallant Will," "The Drinking Song," "The Bridge," and
    "Tent. . .ing,"
That he, so full of *verve* and dash, so wedded to his corps,
Would be the one the order named for duty on before !

But even so; and if within that world that is to come,
The shrill note of the bugle-call, the roll and tap of drum
"Assembly" sound, O let us hope to find him ready there,
On "Jeff," as we remember him, with sabre raised in air!

And should assignment there be made to fort, or camp, or field,
And we be called to guard the flag which now his features shield,
O comrades, may it be our fate to wear the "5" again,
And in the charge beside old "Jeff" let loose the bridle rein!

   CAMP McPHERSON, NEB.
     NOVEMBER, 1876.

TO M. D. G.

How I longed to lean over and kiss her
    As she lay in the hammock alone,
With a delicate fabric of Shetland,
    In exquisite *négligé* thrown
O'er a bosom that swelled in sweet measure
    To the pulse of her passionate heart,
While her lips, with their subtle power pregnant,
    Neither closed, nor compressed nor apart.

Like the cleft you have seen in carnations
    Ere their petals in perfume unclose;
Like the crevice you've seen while inhaling
    The delicate breath of the rose,
They lay all upturned and unshadowed,
    Unconscious that covetous eyes
Were watching their vapor-like tremor—
    Faint whispers of Paradise.

I envied the sweet woodland zephyrs
    That toyed with her features and hair!
I envied the grass-netted hammock
    Its burden, so wonderously fair!
And the moon for its boldness I hated,
    In daring to pause in its flight,
To linger in languor above her,
    And kiss her warm lips with its light!

TO M. D. G.

My soul was the field where was waging
   A conflict 'twixt Envy and Love!
My heart was the tenantless arbor
   Opened wide for that innocent dove,
As I longed to lean over and kiss her,
   As she lay in delicious repose,
With a soul pure and white as a lily,
   And lips sweet and red as the rose.

What mortal dare say he is fitted
   To govern a kingdom like this?
What man dare assert he is worthy
   To taste her immaculate kiss?—
Were the thoughts that absorbed me while leaning
   In anguish and bliss where she lay,
While the stars hung in rapture above her,
   And the moon, spell-bound, paused on its way.

To-night in that hammock I'm lying,
   Where I leaned in those dear by-gone days;
No stars light the muttering heavens,
   No moon sheds its lustrous rays;
But the longing, the spell and the passion,
   That held me in thrall in the past,
Still beat in my heart's wild pulsation,
   Still flow in its current so fast.

RETRIBUTION.

He said I was shallow and heartless; that I courted
    attention and praise;
That I showed myself a thorough coquette in all my
    studied ways;
That I cared for naught, save the homage men paid
    at my selfish shrine;
That a generous act and a noble love would shrink
    from a soul like mine.
He told me this in the "German" I led at the "Point"
    that Fall,
And it turned all the sweets that were lisped on that
    night, to the bitterest wormwood and gall;
And I vowed—as I gave him my favor to show I was
    free from pique—
To devote my life to the toilsome task of making
    his proud heart speak!
I vowed, as I pressed my pillow that was wet with
    my angry tears,
To humble his haughty spirit, and silence his scoffing
    jeers!
That on bended knee, with Heaven-raised head,
    clasped hands and yearning heart,

He should swear his love for this "heartless coquette,"
    of his life was its noblest part!
He should swear that before all others, and above all
    on earth below,
Beyond all his wildest visions, ayont all his fancy's
    flow,
That he held me most pure and worthy, most noble,
    perfect and fair,
That I was the queen of his honest heart,—that I sat
    enthronèd there!
Then I'd turn in my mocking laughter (a habit he'd
    always reprove)
And tell him "a shallow, heartless coquette" was hardly
    the thing to love!
And I'd seem surprised he should venture to bow at my
    selfish shrine,
And remind him he'd said that a noble love would shrink
    from a soul like mine!
His cup to the brim and over with a poisonous draught
    I'd fill,
And show him tho' shallow and heartless, I was queen
    of an iron will!
I knew that my task was heavy; I knew that my old-
    time wiles
Would win reproof, as they had before, and now, I
    would gain his smiles.
I knew by his chilling manner, his haughty, triumphant
    air,
That to finish the task I had set me, would require all
    my caution and care!
For he was a dainty subject—fastidious to the
    core!

And I knew it would tax my store of *finesse*, and my
    wealth of artful lore.
He has stopped me at times when singing some song
    that he held as dear,
If one false note of my voice or lute was borne to his
    perfect ear!
And often when dancing, or riding, his critical eye
    would detect
Some trifle that jarred on his senses, and seemed a
    decided defect!
And he ever some fault was finding, and seizing a
    chance to reprove,
And I knew, possessing so many faults, I could not
    inspire his love;
But the barriers reared against me, and the breakers
    I'd have to dare,
Should be razed and crossed by my solemn vow, which
    should bide with me everywhere!

Years have passed, and fulfilled to the letter is the vow
    that I made on that night!
I framed, forged, and fitted the fetter, I fancied my
    wrongs should requite.
Do you deem it has brought me pleasure to witness
    my task complete?
Do you think 'tis a joyful measure that throbs in my
    heart's wild beat?
Do you think that these eyelids bursting in torrents
    of torturing tears,
Or this soul with a passion thirsting, that is quenchless
    through all the years,

Or this brain that is brimmed with madness, or this face that is flushed with shame,
Are symbols that signal my gladness, and joy that I won the game?
O God! what a prize you sent me, had I but the sooner learned!
O God! what a light you lent me, had I not to darkness turned!
But all Thy blessings were wasted. they have left me forever now;
The sweets that my life should have tasted, were drugged by that passionate vow!
The graft I so carefully cherished, beyond my imagining bore;
Its perfume and fruit quickly perished, and to me it but yielded the core.
My heart, soul and brain were freighted with the struggle that filled my life,
Though I saw, ere the conflict abated, 'twas a self-destructive strife.
And *that* is the thought that will harrow my soul till its knell is rung,
For I knew that each poisoned arrow that shot from my venomed tongue
Was piercing the brain that fashioned its barb and deadly aim,
Was piercing the soul impassioned, that strove but to win the game;
And I saw, ere too late, I was waging a war with the one most dear;—
That the enemy I was engaging was loved with a love sincere;—

That the task I was then completing would embitter
    my life to the end ;—
That I was myself defeating, by forbidding my pride
    to bend.
But my senses for action were burning, with the train-
    ing of patient years;
To the Past they were madly turning, and mocking
    my qualms and fears;
And within me a conquering devil that I was powerless
    to sway,
And within me a maddening revel whose tumult I could
    not stay,
Pressed on to the boonless duel, to my suicidal
    doom,
To the siege unjust and cruel, to the door of my
    living tomb!
For those shafts with their fatal mission, that bow with
    its treacherous bend,
Brought death to the fond fruition I saw in my
    triumphing end ;
They had silenced forever and ever the heart where
    my being was held,
And the pride which our lives did dissever, had the
    dirge of my happiness knelled !
And that vow, which was born of resentment uncurbed
    by my girlish years,
Had left for my life's contentment, but sorrow and
    shame and tears !

And now in my cell-like dwelling, by the prison world
    enclosed,

The ghost of the Past is telling the joys that my pride
    opposed ;
It mocks me with hideous laughter, as its skeleton
    jaws unfold,
And shows the Before and after—the dross and the
    precious gold :
It parts with its bony fingers the mist that had veiled
    my eyes,
And with demoniac glee it lingers, as it catches my
    soul-wrung sighs.
It tells me over and over of the blessings my rash
    vow killed ;
It tells me *he'll* never discover his death had my
    heart's throb stilled !
O that is the king of anguish ! the god of torture
    and pain !
O Death ! am I doomed to languish for aye 'neath
    this galling chain ?
Are the fires of Hell so cheerful that I am denied
    their light ?
Is the cold grave shamed and fearful to fold me away
    from sight ?
Is Lucifer's rack so painless that I am forbidden to ride ?
Is Hades so pure and sinless that I must remain out side ?
Is there not some place I wonder, above, beyond or
    before,
Below, beneath or under, that can hide me forever
    more ?
And silence that Past of horror with a dumbness
    forever mute,
And banish the dreaded morrow, with its burdensome
    Dead Sea fruit ?

INTROSPECTION.

When life with grief is freighted,
When hopes and fears are dead,
When the word for which we've waited
    Can nevermore be said,
We muse on days of gladness
Till our thoughts are filled with sadness,
And our brain is brimmed with madness,
    For joys forever dead!

When life seems not worth living,
When doubts and dreams have ceased,
When from giving and forgiving
    We feel we are released;
We hear our sad soul sighing,
We feel our life-blood drying,
We watch our senses dying,
    We live—yet life has ceased.

When nights bereft of slumber,
When days devoid of rest
Unfold their ceasless number
    As if our strength to test;
We spurn the watched-for warning
That comes with night and dawning,
Till the past and future scorning,
    We turn to death unblest.

INTROSPECTION.

So do we live regretting
The death that doth delay;
So do we live forgetting
    The God to whom we pray!
But ere too late, remember,
Those days of love so tender
May return in all their splendor,
    To brighten all our way!

So should we live unfettered
By Memory's galling chain,
So should we live unlettered
    In bliss akin to pain,
That the kiss we sip to-morrow
Should naught of rapture borrow
From the Past of golden sorrow,
    From the Past of bliss and bane.

Mar not the bud just blooming
With the core of fruit decayed!
Prevent the Past consuming
    The sweets before us laid!
And like a bee, then hover
Where sweets their breath uncover,
And fold us, as a lover,
    While we their hearts invade.

TO N. D.

The East like a young blushing maiden,
   Is robing herself for the day;
The lark with spread wings music laden,
   Is piping his matin so gay;
The roses from rest are unfolding,
   And blending their sweets with the air;
While sun, song and splendor are holding
   A feast on this morning so fair.

But a cloudlet swings loose from its mooring,
   And pilots itself from the shore,
Till it crosses my vision, obscuring
   The light that can dawn never more.
No eye save mine own can perceive it,
   As its anchor sinks into my soul;
No soul save mine own could receive it,
   As it tremblingly sinks to its goal.

So, clothed in this cloud do I wander
   Unto lands that have never been trod,
Leaving all far behind that is fonder
   Than rapture or glory or God!
My heart 'neath thy bosom is lying
   Awake in its animate grave:
My soul from its exile is crying
   For rest from life's turbulent wave.

Though I knew I could never possess thee,
   Yet my soul would not wholly despair;
I refused to entice or distress thee,
   By unfolding my future so bare.
God's law like a gulf, yawned unfeeling
   Between us, obstructing our way;
While our thoughts crossed the chasm, revealing
   The dangers that deep in it lay.

And though Hope now deserts me forever,
   And Fate has my destiny sealed,
I would not this barren life sever
   Since thou hast thy true heart revealed:
For 'tis comfort that cannot be shaken,
   To know that thy heart is mine own!
And that mine—beyond billows forsaken—
   Is crowned on thy bosom's white throne

So in exile I shall not be lonely;
   I will dwell in that realm of bliss
That can come to a life but once only,
   As it came to mine fresh with thy kiss:

TO N. D.

The thought of that bliss in brief trances,
   Now fills with elixir my veins;
Till I'm blind to the world's cruel glances,
   And dead to its merciless pains.

From the sands of my desert I'll raise me
   An altar to God and thine eyes!
And no mortal shall censure or praise me,
   As my prayers from the ashes arise:
And when God in His mercy shall call me,
   And I hasten to meet His command,
May I feel—what ere else shall befall me—
   The fond touch of thy heavenly hand!

May it lie, as I kneel in confession
   At the bar where our sins are laid bare,
So lightly in mine, that Transgression
   Will partially portion its share.
And may I then seek reparation
   For the life made so barren and lone,
By crossing the gulf's separation,
   And claiming thee there for mine own.

R. M.

[MAJOR U. S. ARMY.]

"Sic Volo!"

The youngest, truest, dearest of his corps!
    The Staff's fresh bud, the Army's fairest flower,
    Robbing our lives the grim king Death to dower,
    To bloom above in Heaven's trellised bower;
Leaving us lone, forever ever more.
Lover of Poesy, Life and Light and Song,
    Reach out thy hand, as maiden's pure and white;
    Bend down thy head through clouds of silvery light;
    Drop us a star from thine immortal height,
And show to us this parting is not long!
Give us some sign, some proof more sure than hope,
    That thou now dwellest where the angels dwell;
    Send us some signal saying all is well,
    And that our eyes on those same scenes shall ope.

ARIZONA, 1873.

W. H. B.

[BREVET MAJOR U. S. ARMY.]

"*Stat Pro Ratione Voluntas!*"

What mortal dare say why? It is the fate
  Of those who yet live on to know his heart is still,
  His spirit fled! Why seek the cause or will?
Why strive the greed of grief to gorge and sate
With speculations, born perforce too late?
  "*Be satisfied!*" It is our doom to know that he,
  The brightest, bravest *sabreur* of us all,
In slumber lies beneath the sombre pall!
  His deeds and fame remain; 'twere well should we
  Make them our goal, and curb perplexity!
'Twere well to follow in the path he led—
  Lighted for aye by his undying smile—
  And then if Faith but lingers for awhile,
We'll meet beyond, above, where Death lies dead.

NEW MEXICO, 1875.

DISSOLUTION.

I wake mid the ruins of dreams;
   To a scene most weird and bare;
Before, stretch the sands of once beautiful
      streams;
Beside, hover ghosts of once Eden-lent
      gleams;
   Below, smoulder castles of air.

Through long weary years I had planned
   This realm for a maiden so fair:
By sentries of roses its ramparts were
      manned;
From nightingale's throats were its light
      zephyrs fanned,
   And she was to dwell with me there.

'Twas an elf-land of beauty and love!
   'Twas a realm beyond earthly compare!
It was blessed by the angels who winged
      from above,
And infused their sweet breath in the
      garlands they wove
   For my bride, in my castle of air.

Its moon was a planet that swelled
   Each night to a plenilune rare;
And often in fancy her dear hand I held,
As thoughts of the future triumphantly
      welled,
   And bore me to castles in air.

DISSOLUTION.

Every vale of that realm was sweet!
   Each nook had been fashioned with care!
And now when I fancied my bliss was
      complete,
I behold in the ashes that circle my feet,
   The task of my life lying there.

I bend in these ashes of waste;
   I bow at the shrine of Despair:
My soul on its altar is hopefully placed,
That again I be granted a glimpse and
      a taste
   Of my bride, and my castle in air.

The vultures but answer my call!
   The clouds flash a merciless glare!
And back in the ashes I helplessly fall,
My dream for my requiem, my bride for
      my pall,
   My tomb, my wrecked castle of air.

THE DOOMED STAG.

As I am to be married to-morrow,
   I think it is well I should go
Through my traps, lest the fair one's fond fancy
   Should tend towards inspection also:
Though I've nothing whatever to cover,
   Nor hide, nor destroy, nor conceal,
Still it may save no end of odd answers,
   And make me security feel.

Here's a box filled with old scraps of ribbon,
   All labeled and dated with care;
They were cut from the end of the "streamers,"
   That the girls long ago used to wear;
Here is one of black velvet marked "Carrie;"
   Another of pink, bearing "Rose;"
And a delicate blue, labeled "Marie,"
   And a purple, I know 'twas poor Flo's.

Then come the bright scarlets of Sallie's,
   And the orange and yellow of Belle's,
With the old blue and pink christened "Alice,"
   And the claret chenille of Adèle's.
Here are hundreds of dried, withered rosebuds,
   And ringlets of black, brown and gold;
And *mouchoirs* of delicate light duds,
   Embroidered with monograms old.

THE DOOMED STAG.

And here in this old velvet pocket
    Are six fans, and three ear-rings, all odd;
Five sleeve-links, four rings and a locket,
    And a little gold pea in the pod:
Eight bangles, ten veils and some trimming;
    Twelve gloves, and no two the same size—
Would the fair one suspect me of sinning
    If these trophies should meet her fond eyes?

Here's a box of old photographs showing
    The way that we looked at the Springs,
And others at Rye, taken going
    To the beach with our old bathing things;
And some are in costume, denoting
    Our part in some gay fancy ball;
And others that represent floating
    At the pier, in the Captain's old yawl.

Here's a slipper of dear little Mina's;
    I filled it one night at a ball
With Heidsieck, and drank philopena's
    Regardless of matrons and all.
Here's a glove filled with scraps of a letter
    That Daisy's old guardian once penned,
Declaring he thought it far better
    Our marked morning meetings should end.

Souvenirs, valued trinkets, together
    We've traveled these many long years,
Through sunshine and pitiless weather,
    In laughter and sorrow and tears;

THE DOOMED STAG.

But to-night we must certainly sever,
   The last sad farewell must be said,
And the scenes you recall must forever
   Lie buried with loves that are dead.

Notwithstanding this strange fascination
   To cherish you, still you must go;
And I'll practice the art of cremation,
   And treasure the ashes, you know.
Here goes then! On Love's sacred altar
   I'll have a burnt offering of old,
And grief shall not tempt me to falter
   In this sacrifice, dearer than gold.

Here goes the black velvet of Carrie's,
   Dear girl! crape is now what she wears,
And she's settled down somewhere in Paris,
   Alone with her children and cares.
Here, Rose, goes the little pink streamer
   You gave me that night on the stairs;
Had you thought then, romantic young dreamer,
   Of titles and foreign affairs?

Could I think, my Marie, when I saw you
   In this little knot of pale blue,
That the boards and the foot-lights would draw you,
   And cads would applaud your *début*?
And your purple too, Flora, must perish;
   Poor girl, what a life you have led
Since he vowed to "love, honor and cherish;"
   Now he and the children are dead.

And Sallie's bright colors were fated,
  They captured a fossil D. D.—
Now she has a document dated,
  To capture the children and flee.
And Belle's brilliant orange and yellow
  Were destined her colors to be,
For she fancied a shoulder-strapped fellow,
  Who belonged to the gay cavalry.

Gentle Alice, the veil you have taken
  Forbids you these colors to wear,
Far away in a convent forsaken
  By all save remorse and despair.
It was there on the deck of the steamer
  Poor Adèle gave me this in adieu,
Ah! how plainly this faded old streamer
  Brings the loss of the "*Havre*" to view.

And you too must perish, old pocket,
  With your bangles, and *mouchoirs* and fans;
Your ear-rings, and sleeve-links, and locket,
  And gloves, must give way to the banns.
These pictures are faded and yellow,
  And I fancy they'll have to go too,
They can be of no use to a fellow
  Who to bachelor days bids adieu.

I can't burn this slipper of Mina's;
  I will give it to some one to throw
At the brougham, when the last they have seen us,
  For it prophesies luck, don't you know?

THE DOOMED STAG.

While the dear little foot that once wore it
   Is pressing the soil of old Spain,
And the meetings with Daisy—deplore it,
   Can never be managed again.

It is done! as cremator I've finished
   The task I was doomed to perform;
The fire has my treasure diminished,
   And left me depressed and forlorn.
It would be an odd joke if the fair one
   Was engaged in a similar task;
And the thought is sufficient to dare one
   To quickly run over and ask.

But no; I will not trouble borrow;
   I will fancy her thinking of me,
And counting the hours till to-morrow,
   When forever together we'll be.
So I'm off to the little stag dinner
   The boys have arranged at the club;
And I solemnly swear as a sinner
   'Tis the last—and, by Jove! there's the rub.

'Tis the last, that is morally certain,
   And the dinner's expressly to me;
So o'er sleep I must drop the green curtain,
   For we'll not reach our coffee till three.
If I look rough and "rocky" to-morrow,
   And the fair one is led to inquire,
I shall say it is owing to sorrow
   Felt for friends lost last night at a fire.

A BLOSSOM.

I am thinking again of the time I first met her,
    (That beautiful Blossom which buds did surround ;)
I am saying once more, I can never forget her!
    (Though silent she lies 'neath the snow-covered mound.)
I am tracing again those dear features, now holy,
    (I know not if ever she glanced at mine own ;)
I am kneeling where ever in prayer bend I lowly,
    (Before the "*Hic Jacet*" cut deep in her stone.)

The sound of my voice was ne'er borne to her hearing;
    (Nor accent of hers ever fell on my ear;)
My heart beat the measure of hoping and fearing,
    (Her own pulsed a strain Fate forbade me to hear:)
On the throne of my lips lay her dear name engraven;
    (On the altar of hers all my being was laid ;)
My tempest-tossed heart made her bosom its haven;
    (Her breast was unconscious that port had been made.)

A BLOSSOM.

But thrice, only thrice did mine eyes drink her beauty,
    (At a ball; at a *fête*; in her casket of snow;)
Each time my wild heart robbed my tongue of its duty!
    (But then we were strangers! Could I let her know?)
I loved her and made her in secret my idol!
    (She knew not the worship I paid at that shrine;)
And the thoughts, hopes and fears I was powerless to bridle,
    (But how should she know that such longings were mine?)

At night when all nature was silently sleeping,
    (The last ere that casket forever was closed)
By all—save her spirit—unseen, came I creeping,
    (*Her spirit*, then Death had my secret disclosed!)
I kissed her cold hands that lay clasped on her bosom,
    (Those hands which in life were untouched by my own;)
I laid on her breast the one flower she'd have chosen,
    (But how could she choose when her spirit was flown?)

I mourned many months for that Blossom which perished!
    (Ah, Death! you were cruel to harvest that bloom!)
My heart, soul and thoughts her dear memory cherished!
    (But could she know that, in her echoless tomb?)
Then tell me, why left she this comforting stanza?
    (Found after the daisies had bloomed on her dust)
Ah! where find a Merlin to read me that answer?
    (Her spirit alone with the answer I trust!)

A BLOSSOM.

"When I am dead and all the house is stilled,
When tear-tired eyelids shall be closed in rest,
Then shall the Unknown, whom my heart has filled,
Lay one white blossom on my pulseless breast:
His kingly lips shall press my bloodless hands,
And I shall lie unconscious and unmoved;
But tell him—ere have run the golden sands—
His kiss is felt! and he alone beloved!"

O Death, bear me on to my Blossom, my bride!
  (Come quickly! I care not what form you assume!)
I will mount you unfearing, and recklessly ride!
  (She awaits my approach at the door of her tomb:)
My passion shall guide you! press forward! press on!
  (Ah, Death, you are slow when your presence is sought!)
I feel you! thrice welcome! now let us be gone!
  (Through Death the destroyer, my healer is brought!)

A SCENE IN A CEMETERY.

A body from which the spirit had fled
   Was being lowered to its grave;
Parents and friends with eyelids red
From the scalding tears they dropped for the dead,
Were grouped where the willow and cypress spread
   Their shade o'er the fallen brave.

Apart from the throng kneels a maiden fair
   Enveloped in sombre folds;
A veiling of gloom hides her features rare,
But her heart-wrung sobs speak a keen despair,
And an anguish of soul beyond compare
   For the dead, whom the earth now holds.

In a torrent of tears the maiden kneels,
   As the throng from the grave defile;
Many a glance to that mourner steals—
But she alone knows what that knell reveals,
And the dreadful doom that the Death king seals,
   And the Fate that stamps her "vile."

A SCENE IN A CEMETERY.

'Tis the same old story of trust betrayed,
   That story of Faith and Shame;
Where to stronger man yields the weaker maid,
(A trustful soul, to a heart decayed)
Where a life's the price of the debt that's paid
   By the weak, who must bear the blame!

The throng that follows his flower-decked bier,
   And wreathes his immortal name,
Would deem it a crime she should venture here,
To the sacred ground of their honored dear,
To pollute his dust with her shameless tear—
   If they knew his sin and her shame!

And yet she was pure as the lily white
   Asleep in a woodland dim,
When her idol came in his selfish might,
With his subtle creed of his views of right,
And his vows that his life should her love requite—
   And she yielded through love for him.

'Twas a sin to seek, and a sin to yield!
   A sin that we all should fear;
But to guard the strong with a saintly shield,
And banish the weak to a blighted field,
Is one of the laws that the Lord repealed,
   When He told us to "*Judge not*" here.

But Sin is condoned and Love is condemned
  By this merciless world of ours!
By credulous Faith is the current stemmed
Of that cruel stream, that the soul doth rend;
While laurel-crowned Sin from his throne doth send
  Fresh blights to the blooming flowers!

VIRGINIA, 1881.

RETROSPECTION.

O tell me not that when the heart
    Is filled with grief and pain,
And yearnings for the dear dead days
    Which ne'er can come again,
That Retrospection is replete
    With each enchanting phase,
And brings to you once more the sweet
    Delights of other days!

Ah, no; the Past forever's gone!
    'Tis buried with the dead,
And Retrospection is the ghost
    Of raptures that are fled;
It haunts you with the memory
    Of hours absorbed in bliss,
But does it bring again the sigh,
    The glance, the touch, the kiss?

Does it recall the love-lit eye,
    The tender trembling tone,
The thrilling touch, the honeyed lips
    That once were all your own?
Does it re-fill your vacant arms
    With that fond form again,
And make you see once more those charms—
    Or change to bliss thy pain?

Alas, it tends to change alone
    Your grief to agony!
It makes you feel how wholly gone
    Is all save memory.
The eyes you view are closed in rest;
    The lips are pale and chill;
The form is cold and motionless;
    The hands are crossed and still.

TO B. . B. .

Drifting, steadily drifting,
   Drifting slowly apart,
We who so lately were lifting
   The veil that o'er-shadowed each heart;
We who were drunk with a passion
   That frenzied our blood and brain,
Are drifting, steadily drifting
   Apart on the world's cold plain.

Drifting, steadily drifting
   Wider and wider apart,
Stifling, and starving and sifting
   The life from a soul and a heart;
Leaving us barren of pleasure,
   Leaving us barren of pain,
Drifting our passionless corses
   Apart on the world's cold plain.

To B. . B.

Drifting, steadily drifting
    Farther and farther away,
Borne down the channel of anguish,
    Chilled by its woeful spray;
We, who with veins filled to bursting
    With the blood of a passionate heart,
Are drifting, steadily drifting
    Farther and farther apart.

Drifting, steadily drifting—
    Apart, to the world we appear;
But our hearts and our souls know the secret—
    We are drifting so dear and so near,
That the longings and yearnings they smother,
    And the "raptures and roses" they hide
Will burst with triumphant to-morrow,
    When we drift on Love's isle side by side!

JIMJAM IKE ON REFORMATION.

I tell yer boys, thar's a mine of rot in all this temperance chin!
And I will show how I jumped the claim, if yer'll anchor while I chip in:
Yer must not think that steel pen coats and entrance fee' was my plan,
For that is a blind where the boys stay out to sample the "Valley Tan."
I rasselled with rum for the champion belt that Nick the distiller wore,
And when the jedges hove up the sponge, I'd sandwiched him with the floor!
For I tell yer boys, it's all in the draw, and that anti-temperance plan,
Will bring yer a chowder brimmed up with broth, but nary a sign of clam.
I was raised on the jug in the Sour-Mash State, back in the olden times,
When a feller was jedged by his heft of heart, and the yield of his cobwebbed wines;
When ore was plenty, and four of a kind was reckon'd as safe to "stand,"

When a 30 gait was considered fleet, and bull's-eyes made
    off-hand!
To college I went with the other blocds, whar I worked
    on the Latin ledge,
And picked in the Greek and German lodes, till I thought
    it war time to hedge.
Then I swelled it awhile in a steel pen coat, and kids that
    war soft and white,
And warbled gush to the bong tong girls, till I slipped on
    their taffy—tight.
Then the guv'ner said it war time I quit, and prospected
    round for a claim,
That I ought to draw to some toney profesh, that would
    handle my ancient name,
Well, I drew to the law and caught a Jedge, and I might
    have scooped the pot,
Had I only bet on the cards I held, instead of drawing to
    "rot!"
Yes, fellers; J. Barleycorn got me, and we struggled for
    many a year—
But he tumbled at last to his favorite holt, and threw me
    without a tear;
He used me then as a kind o' bait to gather the blue
    fish in,
And his day-book gave me a credit by pain, and his ledger
    a debit to gin!
I took a whirl at "freeze-out" then with a lot of blue-pill
    beats,
And of all the croppings I ever had seen, they took the
    chromo for cheats!
They'd ante up with a chloral chip, and a swallow of
    bromide tea,

And "blind" with a stack of morphine pills, that would cost yer a "V" to see!
They froze me out, and I struck a trail that led to a big stockade,
Whar the swells retreat to "taper" and "brace," when rum has the mischief played;
But I found that bracing produced a thirst exceeding the former spree—
And ring-tailed monkeys and white-winged rats war the commonest things to see!
I about got even with monkeys and rats, and was going to ask them to shake,
When they changed into wasps with corkscrew tails, and began to bore for my wake:
Still I tapered and tapered, and braced and braced, but before I left that ranch
I'd had the jimjams fourteen times, and missed a bonanza chance!
I rung in then on a pauper claim that was worked by the State on shares,
And lived for a year on herring soup, and the record of bygone "tears."
Old R E Morse just tackled me then with the collar and elbow grip,
And I saw that I either must reef my sails, or scuttle the straining ship;
So I struck a vein whar the color showed, and stuck till the bed-rock gleamed,
And from the wealth of its blessed yield, I never can now be weaned!
I got my health and viger back, and said to the States, I'm done!—

And started in on the Greeley trail to the land of the setting sun.
I flung myself in a buckskin shirt, and let my hair grow wild,
And rigged my top with a brim of felt that would reach for a Yuma mile!
I rented my waist for arsenal grounds, whar Bowies and Colts were hung,
And grafted on that border air, denoting a "son of a gun!"
I found my Greek and Latin lore were cards they could not draw,
So I jammed it down in my boots with my pants, and tackled their wild patwar.
I put up this ranch, and here I have lived since the Spring of '49,
And many a rummy has anchored here, but never a drop of wine.
"Tis here that I grind out the Requiem Mass for the comfort of Whiskey's soul,
And buckskin shirts prove a surer draw than steel pen coats and toll.
Those nails druv into that upper beam just stand for the men I've cured,
And I rekon yer'll find thar's a trifle more than yer steel pen coats have lured!
I tell yer boys, to fetch the Turks yer must do as the turkeys do;
And when fighting the devil yer lose yer grip if yer bite off too large a chew!
Yer should not draw out yer "Green Seal" pouch and ask for a cuspadore,

JIMJAM IKE ON REFORMATION.

When the next man bites from his Navy plug, and aims at
    the knots in the floor!
The claw-hammer coat and ticket plan does well enough
    for the girls;
But temperance talk in a style like that, is suggestive of
    swines and pearls!
A rummy who's pawning his undershirt to buy him a flask
    of gin,
Wont bar the drink and spout the shirt for a ticket to
    hear one chin!
Yer may spring yer pledge, and get him to sign when so
    full he can scarcely write,
But binding him thus from the power to drink, is bidding
    him go get tight:
To tell a rummy he *cannot* drink when he feels a strong
    desire,
Is like telling a hero he cannot fight when you call him
    a sneaking liar!
And to tell the sage of a thousand drunks that a badge in
    his button-hole
Denoting Temperance, is worth the world, just strikes him
    a trifle droll.
Yer must break them in as yer would a colt that never
    has felt the curb,
With a bright loose box and plenty of feed, till they come
    and go at a word;
And yer'll find the cinch they'd have bucked to hell had
    yer buckled it on before,
Will fit like the ball in the rifle's throat, or the ace in the
    faro "door."
Yer must play them awhile as yer would a trout, and
    learn the strength of their hand,

For yer'll lose yer hook and yer rod to boot, if yer yank
 'em too quick to land.
Yer must go to them in their dens and holes, and treat
 'em as pals and pards,
Or yer'll find yer're fresh to the game they play, and
 lost on their style of cards.
If a cuss chips into this temperance pool for the purpose
 of working weal,
And follows the "system" I'm giving away, he can "call
 the turn" each deal ;
But if he goes in for the women's sake, in style, with the
 entrance plan,
He'll pull to a pair till his liver is white, but he never
 will "catch his man ;"
And yer'll find the bulk of the feller's heart who follows
 that kind of game,
Is about the size of a flea's eye-tooth, and the heft of a
 lizard's brain ;
And I tell yer, boys, yer may bet your "stack," when we
 climb the Golden Stair,
Old Jimjam Ike in his buckskin shirt will lead them fellers
 there !

I'll own that back in my younger days I kind o' flew the
 track,
But when I savey'd the race was foul, I waltzed to another
 tack !
And I rekon them nails in that upper beam—thar's two
 hundred and fifty four,
Will go a piece with that MERCIFUL JEDGE, towards barring
 out that score.

To B.

I would not have thee grieve nor mourn,
   Nor have one tear-drop dim thine eye,
When tidings of my fate are borne
   To ears that now in slumber lie.

I would not have thee think or dream
   That any act or word of thine,
Swayed the swift current of life's stream,
   Or urged or caused this act of mine.

I would not have thee sit and brood
   On hours forever gone and past,
Nor when in a desponding mood
   Recall the hours which were our last.

I would not have thee, when the tone
   Of some old long forgotten song
Refills thine ear, sigh "'Twas mine own,
   Sung by his lips, now mute so long."

TO B.

I would not, should the love which now
    Protects thee change, and lie as dead,
Have thee recall an old time vow,
    And muse, "Would *his* so soon have fled."

I would not have thee, should the ties
    Which now enfold thee, rend and part,
To retrospection turn thine eyes,
    And say, "*His* was the truest heart!"

For thoughts like these alone have power
    To make thy sorrow doubly sad;
They'd make more dark thy darkest hour,
    And I would have thee ever glad.

But if some time a thought of me,
    Might bring one half the wild delight
I felt while lingering near to thee,
    I'd bid thee not forget me quite;

And if perchance in gloaming hours
    Some tender spirit in thy feet
Should lead thee on through sylvan bowers,
    Adown the forest's dim retreat,

And guide thee to the shaded mound
    Beneath the tree that marks the spot
Where I lie sleeping in the ground—
    So sound *thy* step awakes me not;

TO B.

Should'st thou, whilst briefly pausing there,
   Shut out the future from thine eyes,
And muse on days more clear and fair,
   And nights of brighter moonlit skies;

And murmur, "O again to press
   My lips to those I loved so well!
Again to feel his warm caress,
   Again to hear him say, 'Dear Belle'!"

If thou should'st see a daisy droop
   Its head, as by a zephyr blown,
Then raise its head above the group,
   And bow again to thee alone,

Thou'lt know my spirit is the flower,
   And that it sways by breath of mine,
And that it strives with all its power,
   To rise again and mix with thine.

Ope then thine eyes—be worldly wise,
   Cut "Coward" and "Fool" upon my stone!
These words can never break the ties
   That hold me, even dead, thine own.

I am not happy from thy side,
   And naught save Death can bring me peace;
"Twould not be Life if severed wide,
   Nor Death if robbed of its surcease.

TO B.

Remember that I happy die,
    For thoughts of thee my being fill;
Thy name upon my lips shall lie
    When all is calm, and cold, and still.

Do as I bid, nor grieve nor mourn,
    Nor have one tear-drop dim thine eye,
When tidings of my fate are borne
    To ears that now in slumber lie.

And then perchance, in other lands,
    Where souls and spirits are at rest,
We'll meet again with out-stretched hands,
    And dwell together, blest.

MARYLAND, 1880.

POVERTY.

'Tis bitter to see them passing away,
   Those dear ones I've cherished so long,
When the sun shines so bright and the world is so gay,
   And the birds fill the air with their song;
But as leaves which in Spring-time are tenderly born,
   In the Autumn must wither and fall,
So they one by one from this bosom are torn,
   Till but one now remains of them all.

And here as I sit in the gloaming to-night,
   With my hand on this little one laid,
I wonder if those that are lost to my sight
   Would return, if I ceaselessly prayed :
I think, could they gaze on this desolate home
   Which once was so joyous and bright,
They'd return to the old one from whom they have flown,
   If only to cheer him to-night.

POVERTY.

I should not complain, for one dear one is left
   To brighten my desolate way;
And though limbs may be shattered, if all are not cleft,
   The trunk should not totter or sway.
Weep not, lest your sorrow should blend with mine own,
   And make me more wretched and weak;
You may dry your moist eyelids, and stifle that moan—
   'Tis of *dollars*, not beings, I speak.

THE DEBUTANTE.

I met her at the "German,"
   The fairest of the fair,
With diamonds trembling at her ear,
   And sparkling in her hair.
I said, "I'd like this 'break' with you,
   If really you don't mind?"
She answered, "Many, many thanks;
   You're quite *too awfully* kind."

Her dancing was perfection,
   Her motion was a dream;
I waltzed her to the supper-room,
   And handed her a cream.
She said, "O thanks, so *awfully* much!
   I'll have some water-ice;
Cream, I *never*, 'hardly ever' touch;
   Thanks, you're quite too awfully *nice*!"

THE DEBUTANTE.

She said, "To loll in supper-rooms
    Is really quite *too* cad !
To lounge upon the stair-way,
    Is not quite *half* so bad ;
And really if you do not mind,
    I think upon the whole
We better find a place there,
    For this is *quite* too awfully droll !"

She said, "Though I'm a *débutante*,
    I know no end of life !
You need not fear to talk to me
    As though I were your wife."
I said, "If I might dare to hope"—
    But here the creature laughed.
And said, "I think you really are
    Just quite too *awfully* daft !"

I intimated that the strains
    Which filled the ambient air,
Were far too sweet to waste in talk
    Upon the crowded stair.
She answered, "Yes, 'tis from the 'Chimes,
    I think it *quite* too grand !
Suppose we dance, just idling here,
    Is quite *too* awfully bland !"

I pinned my favor to her,
    And her fair face flushed with joy,
She said, "I really think you are
    Not *quite half* bad a boy !

And I *dote* upon your calling!"
 I answered that I would.
And then she said, "You really are
 Just quite too awfully good!"

*　　*　　*　　*　　*

As I wandered along in the moonlight,
 I pondered the hours just flown,
And my thoughts strayed back to the dear old girls,
 That I in the Past had known.
Then I entered my club and ordered
 A spiced Jamaica, hot;
And voted the present *débutante,*
 Just quite too awfully rot!

WASHINGTON, 1877.

TO M. C. F.

'Twas midnight, I think, when I heard it;
   It came with a grunt and a wheeze,
Like a mixture of anger and envy
   Rolled up in a sneeze;
With an ugh! and a bulge and a burble,
   And a sort of a kind of a goff!
And a horrible hideous gurgle,
   As if straining to cough.

Just think for a moment of noises—
   Indescribable noises I mean,
Like those you have heard in the pauses,
   When aroused by some sound from a dream;
And of those you have plainly detected
   At night, after going to bed
With a brain by a novel affected—
   A ghost one, just read.

Think of sounds, every kind, hard and soppy;
   Only those though you cannot explain,
Or describe, or illustrate or copy,
   Like tearing *de laine*;

TO M. C. F.

Or that made by the swell minus palate,
   When hailed in the street for a cad;
Or like cracking an egg with a mallet,
   But the egg must be bad.

When two millions of these you've collected—
   The vilest that ever was heard,
Dove-tail and veneer them together
   In one mammoth word;
Then get forty four lantern-jawed vestals,
   And thirty three alley felines,
And a dozen slab-sided Celestials
   From tropical climes,

And make them, at once and together
   In the shrilliest, chilliest tone,
Give vent in the foggiest weather
   To this word of your own,
And 'twill sound like the sweetest sonata,
   Or a symphony—Mozart's in "C,"
To the tomb-like and gollyglup starter,
   That thrilled me while dreaming of thee!

How well I remember the horror,
   The agony, torture and pain
I endured, as I prayed for the morrow,
   And framed firm resolves to abstain
From all sin, and unholy devices,
   Such as poker, and going on "tears,"
And from time thrown away eating ices
   At "Germans," with girls on the stairs.

TO M. C. F.

O ye gads, what relief! day is dawning!
   Now I feel more like perishing game;
I will meet it, alone, in the morning!
   If I kill it, what blame?
But where is it? the room is deserted!
   Still I cannot believe 'twas a dream—
Neither was it! the fiend has just spirted!
   The fiend is the STEAM!

How I hate, how I loathe and detest it!
   How I writhe as I gaze on its coil!
How I long from my chamber to wrest it—
   Its nerve to despoil,
And fling it, this vile apparatus,
   So far from its altar supreme,
That its grunts and its spirts should not part us,
   When of thee I dream.

So I go, thanking God in my going,
   That Fulton and Watt are both dead,
And in Hades are steadily glowing
   O'er furnaces red.
Though that heat to their taste may be dryer
   Than their favorite method of steam,
'Tis a quieter and steadier fire,
   And perchance they may dream!

A QUANDARY.

I know not how I can win my love,
 For she's wedded with one much older;
I know not how I can cage my dove,
 Against all the world to hold her.
For if in triumph I bear her away,
The world—well, we know what the world would say,
And that those who dance must the piper pay,
 Yet these arms so long to fold her!

She's a wonderful love, this love of mine,
 Who is wedded with age and sorrow;
Her presence inspires like a draught of wine,
 And her eyes do the sun's light borrow.
Her—but 'tis needless for me to proclaim her charms,
Or confess the longing that thrills these arms,
Or tell of the tempest her warm breath calms,
 That's born of thoughts of the morrow.

I told her last night, as together we sat
 On a sofa with splendor covered,
While I toyed content with her raven plait,
 And the moon at the lattice hovered,

A QUANDARY.

That—but it matters not what to her I said,
Nor the language I used as my cause I plead,
For you know I told you my love is wed!
   So think of my words as smothered.

Her hand—but no! no!—to her arm was bound
   By a band that with gems was glowing;
Her words which chimed with a silvery sound,
   All her wealth of mind were showing,
As she—but I doubt if 'tis right to tell,
How her soothing words like a prelude fell
To the symphony grand that my fears did quell,
   So this must be all your knowing.

Then—but you will not mind if I leave her here,
   And tell you of how we parted;
How that aged spouse like a ghost did appear,
   As from under the curtain he darted,
And said, "Though I would not be impolite,
I think the *last* car is just coming in sight,
And unless you intend to remain *all* night,
   Perhaps 'twere as well if you started!"

So how can I win this love of mine
   When her doors are barred 'gainst my coming?
Ah! how can these arms my love entwine,
   Is the strain my poor heart keeps drumming.
But I think I will try an original plan,
Which I fear to tell, lest that aged man
Should "drop" on my patent with visage wan,
   And leave her my requiem humming.

A LIFE DRAMA.

She found the sleeve of his morning coat
    Entwined with an amber hair;
And as her own was a dingy brown,
And he had none on his rink-like crown,
    She wondered how it came there.

But her wonderment ceased when the girl came in,
    To see what she'd have for tea;
For she noticed the girl was young and fair;
She also noticed her amber hair,
    And she mentally said, "*I see!*"

Though she never has ceased his coat to scan
    For a mate to that amber hair,
Nor trace, nor a sign to her doth appear;
But then that isn't so *awfully* queer,
    For the girl is no longer there!

And now when you mount those marble steps,
    And give to the bell a pull,
You behold a fiend of enormous size,
With a boneless nose, and telescoped eyes,
    Whose *caput* is topped with wool!

And you'll find, when next with this dame you converse,
    Should your topic be "Races and Rights,"
That ere you have seized on your ulster to go,
The shots she has fired were intended to show
    That the Blacks are far better than Whites!

"COME IN;" OR THE SIX SEASONS.

Long years have gone by since the time when a boy
    I stood in our garden below,
Entranced with delight and enraptured with joy,
    As I viewed my first vision of snow;
As the flakes wavered down in their flickering fall
    As noiseless as that of a pin,
The fond voice of my mother I heard faintly call,
    "Come child, you'll catch cold dear; come in."

Long years have gone by since I stood in our yard
    With a "shinny" stick held in my hand,
Looking on at a fight that was raging quite hard
    'Twixt our boys and a mixed village band.
The stones flew like bullets, the bats and the blows,
    And the screams made a deafening din,
Still the voice of Jack Austin distinctly arose,
    Saying, "Skeesicks, peel off and come in."

Long years have gone by since the time when I tapped
    At the door of her *boudoir* of blue,
And my heart beat with joy as I fervently rapped —
    In the manner that loving hearts do;

When the door quietly swayed, by a motion unheard,
    And an angel—ah! dream not of sin—
In a voice sweet as notes of a twittering bird,
    Said, "Why, Skeesicks, my darling, come in."

Long years have gone by since in Julesburg I strayed
    Through a portal of darkness and vice,
Where a gang of rough men at a bar were arrayed,
    Apparently playing with dice;
The scene was not tempting; I turned to withdraw,
    When a scout said, "We're tossing for gin!"
Then turned, and advancing said, "Stranger, yer paw;
    You've sixes to beat; but come in."

Long years have gone by since the time when I sat
    In a tent on the Laramie plains,
Playing "draw" with the boys, who with rhino were fat,
    Having come from the "Hills" with their gains.
We were playing jack-pots, and no one drew a pair
    Till the pool grew a fortune to win,
When Jim softly murmured, "I'll open it square!
    And Skeesicks, old pardy, come in."

Long years have gone by and my sight's getting dim,
    I am nearing what cometh to all!
Wrap me up in my blankets and warble the hymn,
    Beginning, "He came at each call."
I'm going! What is that? 'Tis a banner of fire,
    And on it in blood written "SIN!"
'Tis Old Nick himself bears it! who says, "We'll retire;
    What, Skeesicks! old victim, come in."

THE MEADOW-LARK.

A little lark lit by a bung while dry,
And he twittered a cry, "I'll try, I'll try!"
 Then he jumped in the hole,
 And swallowed the whole
Contained in that barrel marked "RYE," rye, rye,
Contained in that barrel marked, "RYE."

Then the little lark up through the hole rose he,
And he twittered a cry, "Drunk-y, drunk-y!
 I will brace me and fly
 To a field of this rye,
And there shall my little nest be, be, be,
And there shall my little nest be."

So the little lark braced, and endeavored to fly
To a field that was blooming with beautiful rye;
 But the liquor he'd drunk
 Made the little lark funk,
And he fell in a meadow near by, by, by,
Fell drunk in a meadow near by.

THE MEADOW-LARK.

The raven—made famous by Edgar A. Poe—
On that very same eve essayed "bumming" to go,
    But he gasped in surprise,
    When the sight met his eyes
Of a lark in a meadow laid low, low, low,
Of a lark in a meadow laid low.

A crane—'twas a sand-hill one—cantering by,
The intemperate lark in the meadow did spy;
    The crane shrieked in pain,
    "Gad! I've got 'em again,
For a *lark* in a *meadow* is lain, lain, lain,
For a *lark* in a *meadow* is lain!"

At a caucus of birds held that eve at a wake,
The raven and crane both arose and bespake
    The astonishing view
    Of a lark bathed in dew
In a meadow with nothing to take, take, take,
In a meadow with nothing to take.

The caucus invoked all the winged fiends of night
To aid in explaining this marvellous sight:
    Then stilled was each tongue,
    When an old crow here sprung
The remark, that the beggar was tight, tight, tight,
The remark that the beggar was tight.

This happened in ages of floods, Noahs and arks;
But down to this day have these same meadow-larks
  Continued to "Go,"
  And the words of the crow
Head the list of clairvoyant remarks, 'marks, 'marks,
Head the list of clairvoyant remarks.

Should you deem this a fable or day dream or lie,
I beseech thee at dawn seek some meadow and try;
  And you'll find that sweet note
  On which girls and bards dote,
Is simply, "O Rye-y, rye, rye, rye, rye!"
Is simply, "O Rye-y, rye, rye!"

PARODIES.

PREFACE.

It is a common grievance to hear persons complain of having their favorite poems parodied. They assert that it robs the original of its beauty, and that the travesty occupies the place in their thoughts which the poem once held.

I am unable to comprehend this prejudice; were I not, I should not have selected such poems as Story's "Cleopatra," Poe's "Annabel Lee," nor General Lytle's "I Am Dying Egypt!" to parody; for, in my opinion, they are gems in the tiara of Poesy. I could as soon understand a chromo after Angelo or Raphael robbing their work of its beauty and strength, as I could comprehend burlesques of these poems diminishing in any way their immortal loveliness. To me a parody only adds to the merit of the original, for the worthlessness of the former brings into greater prominence the merit of the latter; and while holding such opinion, I should not be expected to apologize for what, if I held different views, would appear not unlike sacrilege.

P. L.

PROLOGUE TO "SLIM BUTTES."

Lest the bright eye of graduating "sub.,"
Fresh from the classic shades of famed West Point,
Should fall upon the ode yclept "Slim Buttes"
And fail therein its meaning to discern,
I fain would bid him ponder well this proem,
And learn from one who sniffed the battle's smoke,
How that great field was fought and won.

As one, when peeping in his partner's hand
Beholds three kings, will glibly "pass,"
So I must pass o'er scenes forever dead,
And tell you only of that gory day.
I long to linger and describe the scene
Wyoming witnessed on the sunny morn
Its troopers gathered on the vacant plain—
Clad in their scouting gear, with saddles packed—
And passed, with well dressed ranks,
In bold review before their dazed Inspector!
"Not much to see," you say. Well, no, not much;
But still so much, that had I but the power
Of that great bard, who carols forth so sweetly
Of the deeds of Arthur and his Table Round,
I'd picture here a scene 'twould wither you!
For when the column's head had gained the point
From whence it started, the bugle-note commanded
"Trot;" and once again before the dazed Inspector

Passed that gallant band. Again the column's
Head had reached its starting point; again the
Bugle sounds; this time the "charge!" and by the
Dazed Inspector, troopers dashed with reckless fury;
Their sabre arm was raised above the head, and
Each hand grapsed with deadly grip that weapon
Known as Colt's new "45;" and as they neared
The crazed and dazed Inspector, each Colt was
Brought unto the felt hat's peak, and then the
Arm was lowered in proud salute! Such was the
Order of the Commandant, who improvised new
Tactics for the field, and put them into practice
On the morn he sallied forth to meet the hostile foe.

 I pass, pass, pass; but fain would linger still,
And tell you of the scenes that Hat Creek viewed
When news of Custer's fate was borne to camp.
I fain would linger, but must needs proceed;
For should I picture here how one, at dawn,
(A dragoon sub.) essayed to clear the stream
From bank to bank, and landing in its centre
Slowly sank, until his bloodshot eyes alone
Were visible; while "dough-boys" on the other
Side ran wild, and from his slumbers roused the
Commandant, to tell him what the daylight had
Revealed—"A dhragoon *loo*tenant, mired in the
Muddy strame!" Or should I tell how Jack and
I at midnight's height meandered slowly forth
From "Beauty's" tent, beneath a moon—the
Moon that night was full—and saw, strung loosely
O'er a wicker chair which stood before the Colonel's
Guarded tent, a canteen of the quartermaster's mold;
Whereat we paused to slake our fevered thirst:

Jack raised the chalice to his eager lips, then grimly
Smiled, and said: "Ye gads! 'tis *rum*!" And rum it
Was; but when the slumbering Colonel rose at dawn,
And sought to brace his nerves, he found a
Ministering angel had his beaker kissed, and changed
Its contents into Adam's ale!—For should I picture
Here such scenes, the saintly subs. of these our later
Days, would close their ears in disciplined accord,
And shriek in shrill falsetto "Crucify!" So now
I pass; but where the band a junction formed
With C——, on Goose Creek near the mountains
Where it heads, I'll raise the blind and play the
Cards I hold.

From there, a column formed of foot and horse,
And guides and scouts and friendly bucks, and
Numbering in the thousands unto two, and in the
Hundreds unto quarter score, moved out in grand
Array, with one intent; to butcher Squatting Taurus,
Known to fame as Sitting Bull, the chieftain of
The plains; the same who murdered Custer and
His braves. This expedition, by its Commandant,
Was dubbed at once the great "B. H. & Y."
And in its midst full many a "cit" was seen,
Sent thither by our country's guardian the "free press,"
In quest of news the world to edify. Guided by
Half-breed Frank (who was by marriage ties joined
To the tribe of Taurus) that expedition moved from
Day to day. At length the creek was reached
Where rosebuds blooming on its either bank give
To the neighboring vale its fragrant name, and there
The trail of Taurus was descried so broad and plain,

That blind men on an inky night conld follow it.
Through endless rain, with rations so reduced that
What was once deemed but a trooper's share, then
Had to serve for four or even five, the column day
By day moved on the beaten trail which led it to
The broken, fretted banks of Yellowstone's dark,
Muddy, turbid stream ; and there the trail was lost
Beneath the wave. (Or so said Frank the half-breed
Guide, who was, remember, wed to Taurus' tribe.)
  June was just budding when we left our posts ;
August was blown when we that point did reach.
That spot, oasis like, rose on the desert of that dreary
Scout ; for there another column on errand similar
To ours (and there ceased similarity) was also camped.
Their tents were pitched ; their blankets dry ; their
Food was nourishing : and from that brave and
Gallant band we begged and borrowed life's necessities.
A steamer plied upon that turbid stream, and those
Worn out by hunger and fatigue were placed thereon
And shipped as baggage home. Among that crowd
Were plainly visible the wizened features of those
Scriveners—those heroes of the "Independent Press"—
Who there upon the steamer's crowded deck waived
Their adieux, and said : "Farewell my boys ! Your
Country's ears shall ring with knowledge of your
Hardships ! We're off ; adieu ! adieu !" From there
That prince of scouts, that monarch of the plains,
"Buffalo Bill," departed too. 'Twas not fatigue nor
Fear that prompted him to leave ; but pure disgust
With C——s' mismanagement, and wrath at being
Led thus fruitlessly by half-breed Frank ; who was,
Remember, wed to Taurus' tribe.

Think not my adolescent sub. our country's ears
Were doomed to ring with knowledge of our sufferings;
For when those mighty monarchs of the quill had
Reached their homes, and donned their dressing-gowns,
And slipped their feet in slippers lined with down,
They penned their letters to the world at large,
Omitting reference to our hardships and condition,
And *praising* him whom they so lately damned!
They all had fled with two exceptions; those
Remained and saw us to the end; but even they
Refrained from whispering in our country's ears
The farce enacted on those Western plains.

Again the column moved. Its destination was the
Fort named after him, that mighty chief, who fell
By murderous hands in Washington. But when
The point was reached where we our course should
Change to reach the fort, our leader, that benighted
Commandant, conceived a plan, which for stupidity
Exceeded all the blunders made before. 'Twas this:
To cross the Bad Lands to the "Hills," and lend
Protection to the miners there!—His obvious reason
Was to win the praise of those frontiersmen, who
Would laud his name. And so our course was changed;
The fort abandoned for the Black Hills' aid.
Rain, rain, increasing, endless rain! Day after day,
And night succeeding night, we plodded on through
Mud that reached our knees, and slept in pools
Of water, cold and chilled. No tents had we;
No covering save the solitary blanket which the
Order licensed us to bear, and that weighed down
With mud and rain and filth. No rations save one

Hardtack now and then, and slices cut from our poor
Worn out steeds, as day by day we butchered them
For food.   No fuel but the damp grass fanned to blaze,
To cook this loathsome steak, and which we had to
Salt with powder from our belts.   Coffee and tobacco
Gone! And so we moved; *we*, whom the politicians call
"The Nation's Pets," and whom the papers dub "The
Epauletted Aristocracy," moved day by day, over the
Bad Lands to the distant "Hills;" guided by half-breed
Frank, who was, remember, wed to Taurus' tribe.

At length a point was reached where the benighted
Commandant and half-breed guide a consultation held,
Which terminated in the mild intelligence that we,
"The Nation's Pets" were *lost!*

Then from the Third some sixty men were picked,
And officered by five as gallant men as ever buckled
Spur or drew the blade, and sent in quest of frontier
Settlement, known to exist somewhere within the "Hills."
That very night that little band beheld the towering
Lodges of the hostile Sioux.   At early dawn the
Village was attacked; the inmates all were routed,
Captured, slain.   The pony herd (I think two
Hundred head) was also counted in as blessed spoils.
That was Slim Buttes! and to that little band *alone*
Belongs the glory of that day!

By noon we all had reached the scene; the fight
Was o'er; the field was won.   No Indians could be
Seen; but in a ditch, or rather crooked ravine, some
Few were hid, and from that place they fired at intervals.

'Twas there that "Buffalo Chipps," that trusty
"Pard" of Cody's, fell; and several troopers shared
Alike his fate.   Then moved the mighty brain of

That great Commandant: another plan was laid:
'Twas grand! Ay! even Napoleonic. 'Twas this;
To fill two saddles full of dry lodge-poles; to then
Invert two saddles over these; then bind the whole
As if one solid log; to then ignite each end, and
Throw this patent hell into the ditch where foemen
Lay concealed. His object simply this; to smoke
Them out. Sublime! Sublime! But who the
Luckless wight to pack this burning brand across
The open plain until the ditch was reached,—a
Splendid bull's-eye for the hidden foe? And what
Should force the smoke to linger in the confines of the
Ditch when Heaven's blue sky remained its only roof?
Conundrums like to these, propounded audibly by
Bugler boys, convinced the Commandant it would not
Work. He then essayed to charge the ditch! and for
That service picked his chosen few, viz. A pay-
Master, some packers, scouts and aides! they
Soon discovered that was not their *forte*.

While lost in thought, a squaw arose from out
The ravine's depths, and boldly headed for the
Commandant. He siezed her hand and said, "Now
If you'll yield, the Government again will succor you."
She yielded; and the day was won.

The sun showed signs of sinking to its rest,
When from the neighboring bluffs some shots were
Fired, aimed at our herd, which hobbled, grazed
Below; but they were soon corraled; and then till
Darkness fell upon the scene, a scattering interchange
Of shots was sent up from our camp, and down
From adjacent bluffs. With what result? you ask;
Well, seek the Commandant's "Report," and there

You'll find his number of the slain. We who did the
Firing say *thirteen!* But then, perhaps the Commandant
Included *canines* in his estimate ; if so, his figures
Might be multiplied.

Next day the ponies' lives were sacrificed: we closed
Our eyes, and fancied we ate veal.

Again the column was in motion—straight for the "Hills."
But ere the rearmost file had moved four hundred yards
From where we camped the previous night, three
Hundred warriors daubed with their war paint,
Armed to the teeth, and eager for a fight, poured
Volley after volley in our midst ; but *we* pressed
Onward to "protect the Hills."

There was a chance to fight ! There moved two
Thousand men with backs to foe, while in each
Bosom pulsed a heart that beat with hope to hear the
Buglers sound the "charge ;" but no ; our gallant
Commandant decreed no shot from out our ranks
Should backward go ! So, guided by half-breed
Frank, who was, you know, a relative of Taurus'
Through his squaw, we reached the "Hills," a starved,
Disgusted crowd. Such was the scout our great
Centennial year was doomed to witness on our
Western plains. Such was the gallant fight yclept
"Slim Buttes," which brought fresh laurels to the
Commandant. Such is the chief whom now the papers
Praise, and dub, "Intrepid slayer of the Sioux !"
But you will notice when the —d. and —th. and —d. horse,
And —th. and —teenth foot together meet, they always
Speak of this affair in undertone, and mention it as
"C——s retreat from Slim Buttes to the Hills !"

June was just budding when we left our posts ;

November bloomed when we our quarters gained.

Now novice, should you live when I am gone,
And when that Commandant has ceased to breathe,
And when a grateful country seeks to rear a fitting
Shaft above his sacred dust; I bid thee gather
From those barren plains, and from the dreary
Cañons of those "Hills," the bones of the poor
Men we buried there; the bones of those starved
Men who strayed from camp, and never more were
Seen save by the wolves; the bones of those worn
Steeds we killed for food, and throw them on the
Grave of that great chief, as fitting token of
His warlike deeds. Then raise the head-board of
A bedstead old (a neat, suggestive form of monument)
And paint thereon this glorious epitaph:

"'Twas in the crimson ides of '64, upon the
Anniversary of the day that's honored for the birth
Of Washington, that he who sleepeth here, was
Slumbering in his bed at Cumberland. Surrounded
By ten thousand boys in blue—eager and anxious
For the coming fray—he slumbered! And when
Morning dawned that band was headless! He, its
Chief, the one who sleepeth here, was captured by
Some *thirty* of the foe, and taken from his couch—
O shameful sight!—and mounted with a "Grey-back"
On a horse, and driven mutely through his guarded
Lines away to Richmond. The "kiotes" pausing at
This motley pile will spare the frame of this departed
G——, as rigidly as they would the bones of the
Immortal one;—but for reasons quite dissimilar.

PROLOGUE TO "SLIM BUTTES."

Now turn to "Slim Buttes," and if failing there
To find a faithful picture of the siege, reproach
Me not, for I that ode revere! It won for me the
Title "Lariat." 'Twas scrawled upon the cover of
A box, while seated in a cañon of those "Hills,"
And two centurions of the —d. and —th. gave me
The name to which I fondly cling.

If memory failed me not, I'd reproduce that princely
Idyl, penned by a gallant hero of the —d. and based
Upon the glories of that siege; but you will doubtless
Stumble on it soon, for horsemen keep it in their
Quarters, framed. And I have read how Navy men—
Those warriors of the sea—have oft been heard to
Lisp it to the Night, while Lurlei-maids poised lightly
On the yards to hear.

SLIM BUTTES.

At Slim Buttes neath the noonday sun,
After the 3d. the fight had won,
Came C—— and pack-train on the run,
    To jump the captured property.

But Slim Buttes viewed another scene;
For close by, in a deep ravine,
Three bucks and several squaws had been
    Firing with great rapidity.

'Twas then each crow-bait charger neighed,
And said, "I'm d——d if I'm not played!"
And G—— C—— like a *burro* brayed,
    Portraying his identity.

Then several faint attempts were made
To charge with C——'s blood-red brigade;
But pay corps, packer, scout and aide,
    Fell back with great agility!

'Twas then a squaw drew near the band,
And C—— advanced and siezed her hand.
And said: "Now yield to my command,
    And I will go security."

The squaw confessed that she was beat,
And that it was a great defeat;
This nobly aided C——'s conceit,
    And proved his capability.

'Tis o'er! The squaw surrendered flat;
C—— penned despatches neat and "pat;"
While half-breed Frank and *petit* Batt
    Sought scalps with great cupidity.

'Tis morn: the ration fight is o'er.
Two hundred pups lie sick and sore;
The ponies' flanks are gushing gore,
    To stimulate humanity.

Few, few are left who care to tell
How starved men cussed and ponies fell;
"Old C—— is right!" the papers yell,
    To G——e's great felicity.

ANTONY.

[AFTER STORY'S "CLEOPATRA."]

Here, Fonteus, fill my meerschaum,
    The one that I won at pool;
And bring me some absinthe and seltzer,
    And see that they both are cool:
Open the window wider,
    And raise me a trifle, so
I can breathe the delicious aroma
    From my garden of mint below.

I dreamed I sat with my Cleo.,
    On a sofa of silk and gold;
But I woke when the vision was sweetest,
    And the secret can never be told;
It has gone from my mind like some stupid
    Engagement I purposely broke,
And the sofa and Cleo. have vanished
    In a cloud of perfumed smoke.

Squirt on me attar of roses
    From that tube on the bracket there,
And pour a few drops of the "Duchess"
    On my face and *moustache* and hair;

Go get your comb, and play me
    A suicidal tune,
To rhyme with the dream that departed,
    And awoke me, alas! too soon.

There, drowsing upon the afghan,
    Stretches my deer-hound "Fan,"
And rests her neck on the shoulder
    Of my sleeping setter "Dan."
The mouser yawns on the divan,
    And opens his mouth to enfold
A fly that is dead with slumber,
    As into his mouth 'tis rolled;
The air is too hot and sultry
    To venture to move or stir,
And the clouds are as still and motionless
    As the frame of a strychnined cur.

Ye gads! this endless *ennui*
    Is wearing my life away!
O for a row and ruction,
    With bullets and slugs to slay!
Throw down that comb—I loathe it!
    Take your silver trumpet instead,
And sound out the "Stable Call Waltzes"
    To awaken this world so dead.

Hark! to my broncho beauty—
    My *burro*, yellow and white,
With ears like a trowel-bayonet,
    As they stand on parade at night.

Look! listen! as higher and higher
  His head in the air he rears,
How he reaches, with neck uplifted,
  And brays as he flaps his ears!
O *burro*, bray for Cleo!
  Bray, "Come to me, love, awhile!"
Bray, "Cleo! Cleo! Cleo!"
  Till she hears you down by the Nile.

There—leave me, and take from my chamber
  That stupid pet of a lamb,
She drives me half distracted
  As she bleats for her distant dam!
Take her,—she makes me nervous—
  And fling her into the street,
Or, by the ghost of Octavia's cat,
  I'll can her for potted meat!

Leave me to gaze on the fashions
  Thronging the streets and squares,
Where the Summer sun shines sweetly
  On the world with all its cares;
Till an ominous cloud in the westward
  Bursts in a torrent of rain,
And absorbs, as a sponge in a basin,
  Each new grenadine and gros grain;
And the skeleton frame of the bustle
  Has lost its haughty mien,
As it droops like a last year's lily,
  Distorting each gore and seam.

I will lie and muse on the old times,

That have passed like a dream away,
And with chloral, absinthe and hasheesh
　Madden my fancy to play;
When, a grey and yellowish "kiote,"
　Mixed with a little dun,
Softly and swiftly footed
　I wandered, where never the son
Of a white man nor Greaser nor Indian
　Had planted his mighty heel,
And, wild in a reckless freedom,
　I started some grub to steal.
The gopher dug like lightning,
　So dreadful was his fear,
And the vultures left their carcass
　When they spied me creeping near.
I gulped down the choicest portion
　I found upon the plain,
Then screaming, barking and yelling.
　Jumped in delight again,
Till I heard my wild bride wailing
　In the depths of a cañon near,
Which meant, in the language of kiotes,
　"Come love; you have nothing to fear;"
Then I screamed, and yelled in answer,
　And shook my coat in pride,
And off like a rocket started
　To fondle my wild young bride.
We spooned in that dismal cañon
　Beneath a *mesquite* tree,
And snapped at each other our lantern jaws—
　'Twas a jaw-yous sight to see!
Her white eyes looked like snow-balls

As she sat and winked at me,
And her bushy tail, like a fly-brush,
Fanned the sage bush nervously.
Then like a trap she grabbed me,
With a fierce unearthly groan,
And we met, as two cats in an alley
When a boot-jack at each has been thrown.
We snapped and snarled at each other,
For her love like her lungs was strong
And her teeth from the nape of my scrawny neck
Had often the claret drawn.

Often another she-wolf—
For I was thought quite swell—
Would sit on her haunches winking,
And longing her love to tell;
But Cleo'd appoint her funeral
At the hour we had set to dine,
And at furnishing rival's corses,
Her light was the first to shine.
Then down to the creek we wandered,
Where the prairie-dogs came to stroll;
Like a hurricane we jumped them,
Ere they'd time to reach their hole.
We drank their blood and crushed them,
And picked them clean to the bone,
And six of the bravest decided
That Cleo. could whip them alone.

Those were the clothes-pins we were!
None of your common kind,

With their puny, petty passions,
    And "mimsy," maudlin mind!
No nonsense about the future,
    Nor the thought of what folks might say,
Disturbed in the least the glorious life
    We lived in our rollicking way.

Come to me, Queen, I'm longing,
    The sun in the West is gone;
And the kiote's old time fury
    Through my veins runs quick and warm.
Come not sneaking to steal me!
    Take me with sand and shell,
As dredgers do the oyster!
    I will not scream nor yell.
Come as you came in that cañon,
    Ere we to humans were turned,
When the kiote's fury was in us,
    And love in your optics burned!

As soon as I coppered the three and the nine,
   In that hot Ter-ri-to-ree,
A pile of new bills was thrown on mine,
   Bet "open" to win, you see !
And I wondered what youth had a nerve so fine
   As to buck at this game 'gainst me ;
So I turned to see, and flushed with wine
   By my side stood Car-ma-nee—
   My little brown Car-ma-nee !
And the pile of new bills that on mine were laid,
   In that hot Ter-ri- to-ree,
Were the very same bills that to me were paid
   By the U. S. yes-ter-dee—
Paid by the U. S. for scouts I had made
   In pursuit of such raiders as she !

I "savey'd" sufficient to plainly see,
   In that hot Ter-ri-to-ree,
That a fearful job was put up on me
   By the dealer and Car-ma-nee ;
And though I played "low and crafty,"
   (Like the Watsons I seemed to be,)
They left me the wreck in reality
   That I in prospective did see !

O for the strength and the "sand" Poe gave
   To that kinsman of "Annabel Lee,"
To aid me in bearing her off to the wave
   And dropping her into the sea !
Not any white sepulcher in mine
   At the planting of Car-ma-nee !

A bag with stones to the number of *nine*,
  Is a swell enough send-off for me.

Now the moon never shines
  But I see threes and nines·
Gazing down in derision on me,
  And the Night does not pass
Without murmuring "ass,"
  In the lingo of Car-ma-nee;
And the star never shoots, but I swear the galoots
Who put up that job shall yet die in their boots;
  The dealer and Car-ma-nee!
  Deplorable Car-ma-nee!
That she should cry "*Bueno!*" when viewing the wreck
  Her Greaser job made of me!

CAR-MA-NEE.

'Twas years, but how many I now forget—
   In a hot Ter-ri-to-ree—
That a Greaser lived; and you can bet
   That her name was Car-ma-nee;
And this girl pretended her only wish
   Was to spoon, and be spooned by me.

I was as wild, and she was as wild
   As a parentless hawk might be;
But we spooned with a spoon, by the big-horn spoon,
   I and my Car-ma-nee—
With a spoon that the great spoon king, Butler,
   Coveted her and me.

So this was the reason I called one day
   At the ranch of my Car-ma-nee,
Where her *madre* greeted me with, "*Usted
   Buenos dias, si-en-tc-se*;"
And said: "*Senorita*, she gone take walk
   With her pet pup 'Skim-ma-zee,'
In hopes of meeting and having a talk
   With her dear *Ten-e-an-te.*"

The fellows, not half so happy in camp,
   Went envying her and me;
And this was the reason she took that tramp,
   In that hot Ter-ri-to-ree,
Simply to show them her vestal lamp
   Was burning alone for me;
At least, in this manner I put the thing up,
   (For conceit had the better of me,)
As I strolled along through old Tucson,
   In quest of my Car-ma-nee.

For our love it was stronger than Limburger cheese,
   Or the love of folks greener than we—
   And of many far slower than we—
But neither the ghost of old loves gone before,
   Nor of those in prospective I see,
Can ever induce me to trust any more
   In my little brown Car-ma-nee!
For there on the *plaza* I found her engaged
   In that villainous game, *mon-te!*
She was bucking the ducats I gave her for clothes
   Away at that game, *mon-te,*
And betting her *alse* and my *pesos*
   Away on some Greaser "pre."

I saw if this Greaser continued to play
   A financial wreck I would be;
So I slid to a booth, in a priestly way,
   And coppered the nine and three,—
Bent only on making a "stand-off"
   With the loss of my Car-ma-nee.

TO M. C. W.

I am dying, Army, dying!
    Freely ebbs the crimson gore;
And some other "sub." will glory
    When he learns I am no more.
Let thine arms, O "Judge," support me!
    Close thy commissary jaws;
Listen to the things I tell thee,
    And too soon thou'lt learn the cause.

Though my chief, the *Nan-tan-in-cha*,
    Dared to say I played it ill,
When I drew to two small *targies*
    On a "pre" that I should "fill;"
Seek him, say old Hoyle hath sent thee
    To applaud that master stroke;
That my cheek with science mingled,
    Never more should see me broke.

Though my raw, untutored "C" troop
    Wear their felt hats never more;
Though my vouchers for September
    Still have sunk a little lower;

TO M. C. W.

Though no *nad-a-lins* surround me,
  With *coon can* to lure me on,
I shall perish with the comfort
  That my "Guard-mount" work is done.

Should the troop, when I'm departed,
  Mock the sub. that's laid so low,
'Twas no Tonto's arm that felled me,
  'Twas a *burro* aimed the blow!
He, when Tar-tig-y had left me
  That I flew to in despair;
He, when Zuni had bereft me,
  Sent me beyond need of care.

And for thee, my blear-eyed *Loco!*
  Don-judah! outcast of the band;
Come again beseeching *pesos*
  With thy *mescal*-tinted hand.
Give the *indays* frequent chances
  To efface that Grecian nose,
And in peace I'll *hish-hash mucho*,
  Trusting thee to bore my foes.

I am dying, Army, dying!
  Hir-she! hear old Pedro's band!
They are coming—quick, my sabre!
  Let me feel it in my hand.
Ah! no more when *sol's chiquito*
  Shalt thou don the female garb;
Councils, Boards and Courts shall guard thee—
  Tudle-ki-a! Fatal barb!

THE IRON-BOUND BUCKER.

How fresh in my mind is my old Texas broncho,
    Though long years have vanished since last he was seen ;
That pert, pinto pony my *dulce* named "*Ponco*,"
    Which cost me great *pesos* way out in Tom Green :
How patient he'd stand while you "cinched" up the saddle,
    Never moving a muscle for fear of ill luck ;
How blandly he'd turn to make sure you were straddle,
    And then, O *Caramba!* how vilely he'd buck !
        That old Texas broncho
        My *dulce* named "*Ponco*,"
        And I christened "Donko"—
        Ye gads ! how he'd buck !

How well I remember the day I neared Austin
    To witness a mammoth militia parade ;
I paused to scrape off the red mud I'd been tossed in,
    And bandage the bruises my broncho had made.
How proudly he paced down the desolate by-way,
    Such thorough-bred action ! such proof of good "chuck !"
Till he joined with the throng in the banner-hung highway,
    And then, O *carajo!* but didn't he buck !

How vividly clear in my mind is the morning
   We passed through the portals where Santa Fé gleamed;
The brown *señoritas* in white robes were thronging,
   And on towards the *plaza* the fair column streamed.
I learned 'twas the great *Corpus Christi* procession—
   I might have learned more had I met with good luck—
But just as it neared me in solemn succession,
   That infidel broncho in ecstasy bucked!

How well I remember the motion that thrilled me,
   As over his withers I shot like a ball;
How well I remember the target that stilled,
   Reared high by those virgins to lighten my fall.
How vivid and bright gleams that routed procession;
   How ghastly pellucid, my horrible luck;
But O what gleams brightest,—I'll make the confesson,
   Is the dynamite motion attending that buck!

I am certain the beast was enchanted by witches;
   For during the Summer I claimed him my own,
He bucked me clear out of my corduroy breeches,
   And jostled the teeth in my upper jaw-bone!
He would shut his four legs like a fan close together,
   Then arch his short back, like a moon that had struck;
Then draw down his head to the cactus-crowned heather,
   And centre his energies all in that buck!

It would come with a swiftness that down through all ages
   Will rankle with envy the scientist sage;
It would come with a force that no wizard presages,
   And with a precision no power could assuage.

Should the telephone sharp, or the cable inventor,
    Desire to engirdle the earth, *a la* Puck,
They need only decide to make "*Ponco*" their mentor,
    And blast all their batteries off on his buck.

I swapped him at last to a withered *señora*,
    For a mammoth-eared *burro*, whose habits were known;
But he bucked her from Vegas way down to Sonora,
    And he didn't half try, as his record has shown!
I know not if Fate to that old pinto pony
    Has brought dire misfortune, or borne him good luck;
But all that I own, 'gainst a cracked *cascarone*,
    I'll bet that this instant he's bent in a buck!
        That iron-bound bucker;
        That copper-rimmed bucker;
        That steel-plated bucker;
        Ye gods! how he'd buck!

AN IDLE.

He sat on his steps at the midnight hour,
   Silent he sat, with his head bent low;
The rain came down in a terrible shower,
The lightning flashed with appalling power,
And struck and shattered the old church tower;
   Still he sat on the steps, just so.

A watchman, hid 'neath an awning near,
   Did mentally say: "Why sits he there?"
The awning responded: "Well, not through fear;"
The pavement answered: "He's out of gear;"
The cobble-stones said; "It is certainly queer;"
   But the man moved never a hair.

Perhaps he was waiting for some one to call;
   Perhaps he was waiting for some one to pass;
Perhaps he was waiting the meteor's fall;
Perhaps he was waiting a tunnel-cloud squall;
Perhaps he was waiting for nothing at all,
   Perhaps he was only an ass.

"IT WAS THE CAT."

A Jay-bird of the Army lay dying in his bunk;
No other Jays were conscious, they had sought their nests while drunk;
But a Meadow-lark perched near him, with a rum-besotted eye,
And gazed with palsied glances on that wretched wreck of rye.
The dying Jay-bird chippered as he stroked the Lark's fond wing,
And said: "I never more shall call for 'straight,' or 'tod,' or 'sling;'
Take these jimjams as a warning to other Larks and Jays,
For Nick has called me down to him, to help him tend the blaze.

"Tell the Larks and Jays who gather at my planting on the morn
To shed no tears, but fill the cup with amber juice of corn,
And drain it to the memory of one who early fell,
And with his chips prepared to cash, skipped with a 'How!' to hell.
Say I struggled with the enemy through long successive years,
Unmindful of the warnings that came with frenzied fears,
And when at last my hand was called, the devil could not 'faze'
The nerve I showed, as down with him I skipped to tend the blaze.

"Tell my sister not to weep for me when Jays go reeling by,
With swollen beaks and broken wings, and blue and blackened eye;
But to look upon them proudly, with haughtiness and pride.
For her brother was a Jay-bird, too, and he a Jay-bird died.

"And say that when the Jews came down, my traps to gather up,
I let them take whate'er they would, but kept my old tin cup;
And in dragoon style I drained it to the memory of old days,
Before I skipped below with Nick, to help him tend the blaze.

"There's *another*—not a sister—you will know her by her style,
By the neatness of her fetlock, by the beauty of her smile;
Just say to her when other Larks and Jays were laid away,
You stood beside the bedside of her dear, devoted Jay;—
That when the sound of Gabriel's horn fell tinkling on his ear,
He said he was prepared to go, and showed no sign of fear;
But never let her think or dream I ended thus my days,
By skipping down below with Nick, to help him tend the blaze.

"Another favor, dear old Lark, I ask before I go,
And that is that you'll have me stuffed, and kept *in statu quo*,
And placed above the mirror behind some West End bar,
So I can glower on Larks and Jays, when they around it draw.
Just give me for a pedestal a dried-up pretzel crust,
And there I'll perch, as did the bird upon old Pallas' bust;
So when the birds come in to drink they'll meet the steady gaze
Of him who skipped below with Nick, to help him tend the blaze."

His twitter ceased, his eyelids closed; his cup fell to the floor;
The spirit of that Jay was LOST—it had not gone before.
The Lark bent o'er his stiffened form, while fragrant beads of rye
Fell with the fury of a storm from out his bloodshot eye.
The stricken Lark perched mournfully, and viewed the solemn scene,
Recalling vividly the sprees on which they both had been;
But never, never'll be it known how long he might have sat,
Had he not heard a sound that caused his flight—"IT WAS THE CAT!"

PEACE POLICY.

Not a sound was heard, not a face turned back,
   As through the cañon we hurried;
In search of the red-skins whose nightly attack
   On the settlers, our slumbers had worried.

We reached the spot where the rancheria stood,
   And quickly the place we surrounded ;
Then our rifles converted bad Indians to good,
   As they from their wickeupps bounded.

No useless garments did they parade,
   But their breech-clouts still clung round them ;
And only the hole that the bullet made,
   Changed the fiends from the way we found them.

Few, and short, were the screams they gave,
   For the bullet soon ended their sorrow ;
And they knew the "kiotes" would find them a grave,
   When we marched away on the morrow.

Lightly we talked of the "killing" just made,
   As we gazed on the wickeupps burning;
But their spirits joined not in the joy we displayed,
   For to hunting grounds they were returning.

But half of our endless task was done,
   When we orders received for retiring;
And we heard the mammoth political gun
   That the Quakers were steadily firing.

Slowly and sadly we marched to our post,
   But no symptoms were shown of complaining;
We wrote not a line, and we made not a boast,
   But we saw where the beggars were aiming.

And now as we witness this terrible drought,
   And muse on the woeful pageant,
We know that each Quaker who "shot off his mouth,"
   Is a bond-holding Indian Agent!

ERRATA.

PAGE 17—heart-striken, should read heart-stricken.
PAGE 88—thy, should read your.
PAGE 124—grapsed, should read grasped.

www.ingramcontent.com/pod-product-compliance
Lightning Source LLC
Chambersburg PA
CBHW022118160426
43197CB00009B/1073